# So, About That Death Cult you Joined?

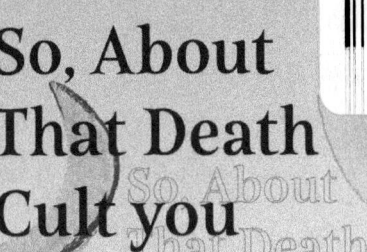

UNMASKING
EMPIRE IN
MODERNITY

NATUREZA
GABRIEL

*Gabriel writes with the fervor of a man saving his own life.*

–James C. Graves

NATUREZA GABRIEL

*praise for* RESTORATIVE PRACTICES OF WELLBEING

"*A remarkable book.*"
–Dr. Stephen Porges, Developer of the Polyvagal Theory

"*An excellent guide to wellbeing and wholeness that is greatly needed today...*"
–Ilarion Merculieff, President of the Global Center for Indigenous Leadership and Lifeways

"*A treasured cookbook for the spirit.*"
–Roshi Fleet Maull, Founder of the Heart Mind Institute

"*...a profound and unique synthesis.*"
–Daniel Rechtshaffen, author of *The Way of Mindful Education*

*praise for* KEYWORDS: A FIELD GUIDE TO THE MISSING WORDS

"*An extraordinary way-finding to what is missing, what has been cut out of the heart of humanity and which can be fully restored by our attention...Gabriel is making our way of being holy again by the quality of attention he brings to the words that are missing, re-storing and re-connecting us with the ineffable so we can re-member ourselves into our ancestral future.*"
– Peter Tarvernise

*praise for* THE NEUROBIOLOGY OF CONNECTION

"*...filled with brilliant trans-disciplinary insights.*"
–Darcia Narvaez, Professor Emerita of Psychology at the University of Notre Dame, Founder of the Evolved Nest

# So, About that Death Cult you Joined?

### UNMASKING EMPIRE

### IN MODERNITY

⊕

ESSAYS BY

## NATUREZA GABRIEL

# So, About that Death Cult You Joined?

NATUREZA GABRIEL

© 2024 Jaguar Imprints & Hearth Science, Inc.

All rights reserved.

No part of this book may be reproduced or transmitted in any form or by any means, electronic or mechanical, including photocopying and recording, or in any information storage or retrieval system with the prior written permission of Hearth Science.

Published by:
Jaguar Imprints
PO Box 567, Nicasio, CA 94946, USA

A CIP record for this book is available from the Library of Congress Cataloging-in-Publication Data

ISBN-13: ISBN-13: 978-1-7362803-9-3

Printed in USA

A note for readers:

The name for this collection arrived after I had designed the cover, which had come to me on the threshold of waking and dream, and was, simply, a mask. At first I thought it was a mask of the *wetiko*, which is an Algonquin word for the cannabilizing monster of modernity (whiteness is infected with this). Later I came across a version of the mask that is on the cover, and when I sat, meditating with this image, inquiring into the title, what came surprised me greatly. Since my bosses keep me informed on a need-to-know basis, I've learned to flow with things I don't understand. As I've continued to work on the book, the reason for the title has become clearer to me.

*There are entire libraries in the annals of medicine about the art of drawing forth poisons from the body.*

# Contents

| | |
|---|---|
| Introduction | 11 |
| 1 • Digging out the Taproot of Supremacy | 19 |
| 2 • On Annihilation | 49 |
| 3 • Inverting the Logic of Enclosure | 65 |
| 4 • Wrong Angles | 84 |
| 5 • Toiling in a Mine | 102 |
| 6 • The Royal Garden | 112 |
| 7 • Death's Head | 125 |
| 8 • At the Origin of Consciousness: A Crime Scene | 129 |
| 9 • Sense-making on the Verge of Collapse | 144 |
| 10 • Sam Altman went to My Highschool | 172 |
| 11 • Oracular Dream | 186 |
| 12 • Automaticities of Sacrifice | 192 |
| 13 • You Ain't Jesus, Bruh | 192 |

Hello
Apocalypse

MOBILE
Item 2 of 2
1 H ICED LATTE
Hot Milk $
+/+ Foam
+/+ Ice
06:27 AM

## INTRODUCTION

# Wherein I gift you Apocalypse

⊕

I was sitting in an Ayahuasca ceremony in an Atlantic forest in the northeast of Brazil, sometime around my 31st birthday. I had consumed a lot of the sacred tea. My inner vision was swimming with fractalized electromagnetic images of dinosaurs unspooling through multi-dimensional space like a hyper-colorized immersive stopmotion film, when it became viscerally clear to me that I was a forest creature. This knowing arrived – I'm not sure whether it ascended to me or descended to me or simply came from another dimension – but I felt it and I knew it in my blood and my bones and their marrow with certainty. It occurred to me to ask why, but the weight of that question across the inner cinemascape was unbearable. The magnitude of reality incoming did not permit the machinations of cognition.

Certain knowings are most properly related to in their facticity. The question of how I came to be a forest creature, is probably, in reality, a 2-million-year-deep question. We all came from the forest it seems, except for certain lineages which came from the stars, or so I am told. This happened so deep in the mists of ancestral memory as to no longer be accessible through conscious thought.

But at that moment, in the ceremony, the question of why was a distraction. That was not the necessary part of what was being shown to me. The eternal plant teacher was showing me who I am. Based on this, it would go on to show me a number of things about my life, which I had, up until that point, been unable to understand. The plant would arrange me, and re-arrange me many many times over the coming years, until I cracked completely apart, and then it would rebuild me altogether. I would come out of this particular experience wanting to be a father. That was something that, going in, had seemed inconceivable to me.

Had I been able, at the time, to articulate clearly why it was inconceivable to me, part of it would have been my own relationship with my biological father, from whom I've been in various states of estrangement and conflict since I left the home of my parents at the age of 18. Another significant part of it would be my concern about bringing a child into the world that I inherited, which, speaking bluntly, is pretty astoundingly fucked up. We have understood, for 40 years at least in modern culture, that we are actively destroying the only biosphere in the known universe. Indigenous cultures have been aware of this for at least 500 years. In 1992, one of my dearest friends presented, at the Rio Earth summit, a crystal clear articulation of this awareness. Since that time, business as usual has continued, which is to say that nothing has been done at an international scale to create the necessary global agreements and enforcement actions that would effectively halt this feverish frenzy of annihilation. Seduced by neoliberal capitalist theoretics, entranced by our own technologies, modernity stumbles blindly and acceleratingly off the edge of a cliff.

We are now in full collapse globally. We are off the cliff. If this is news to you, you're welcome.

The ceremony about which I have been speaking happened in 2006. In 2009 I became a father. When a person becomes a parent, it is not just the child who is born. The parent is also born.

In order to become a father, I had to overcome my nihilism. This was not easy for me to do. I dropped out of Yale University at 19 years old, and was filled with shame about this. My grandfather was something of a functional monster. He was both generous and a grand dissimulator, a serial philanderer, and an incestuous freak. I was the person who disrupted the dynamics in our family system by naming this and revolting. The consequences to me personally were quite severe. I have been more or less estranged from my family of origin since I was in my early 20s. A friend of mine recently used the phrase "the horror of the nuclear family", and I understand deeply what he means.

Thankfully, my early childhood was marked by the experience of being part of a village. The village is one of the most important psychic structures for humanity. Modern people do not understand this at all.

Humans are not designed to be raised by two people. We are not designed to live within the island of a nuclear family. Our deep neurobiology is structured to be nourished by tribe. We, like mushrooms, are designed to thrive in a mycelial network of relatedness.

I couldn't become a father until I reconnected with a tribe, which I didn't know, but the plants did. And in order to reconnect with a tribe, I had to confront my own profound cynicism, which was born of trauma, and of being acculturated into modernity. I had to digest my own alienation. I am using the word digest with deep intentionality. This is some thing that must be broken down into its constituent metabolites. It is at some level a chemical byproduct that must be excreted electrically and chemically, discarded, thrown out, and thrown up.

Alienation is the hallmark of modernity. We could quite effectively view the development of modernity as accelerating deviation from an ancestral baseline in connection and relationship. In other books I have done that, and much of the work that I direct around healing is concerned with this domain.

And so, in order to become a father, in order to open to the possibility of bringing a new life here, to this planet, in its current state, I had to overcome my own trauma.

This was, of course, not a cognitive process. I traveled back to

Brazil while my wife was pregnant, and in a tiny town deep in the Amazon, the name of which translated into English as *Have Faith,* worked through another series of encounters with my own damaged self.

My daughter arrived in August 2009.

While my wife was recovering from a Caesarean section, we found ourselves staying in the hospital for several days. On the second day after my daughter was born, while conducting a routine physical examination, the hospital staff detected an irregularity in my daughter's heartbeat.

I had just been with this tiny being for two days. Her arrival had cracked my heart open, as cleanly as an egg cracks over the rim of a bowl. For two days I had cradled her against my bare chest, while she slept with a tiny fist wrapped around my finger.

When the news came, I went into the tiny bathroom in our room. I could barely bring my attention to a focus, having slept so little, but I prayed to the creator thus: *If you have to take someone, take me instead. She just got here. Let her live.*

It was possibly the first unselfish thought I've had this lifetime.

Within the mystery of things, it turned out that there was an error in the machine, and not with my daughter's heart.

And so, a day or so later, we returned from the hospital to our home as a nuclear family, just born. Nuclear is the correct word.

⊕

I have what I call the 'coffee cup theory' of humans. When I look around at the world, the way people are spending their time, the level of suffering and distraction, the numbness- I have the sense that most people sit inside their lives as though they were inside a cup. Life is just happening, and they're being swirled around by it. Most people don't seem to be able to look out over the rim.

For the middle class folks, of which I am one more or less, the job, a mortgage if they're lucky enough to have a house, getting the kids to and from sports and music practice is what's in the cup. The swirl of life is so great a lot of people don't ever get above the rim of the cup they're inside to look out beyond themselves.

Some of this is physiological: much of modernity is in a defensive fight-or-flight state. In such a state, we're acutely aware of who is with us and who is against us. The circle of our compassion extends all the way to whatever 'us' we have circumscribed.

But sometimes people, through some sort of grace, or spiritual experience, or moments of awe, or authentic connection, or, on the other hand, through rupture–illness, a death, grief, some catastrophe– catch a glimpse of something beyond the rim of the cup. They lift their head up, and look out to what is beyond, and realize that most of what they're doing daily is swirling around in their own private narcissistic haze.

A person might realize this, and experience it as a momentary epiphany. In other cases, if there is some repeatability to this, it can begin to change someone's life and view. To confront some version of the actual world, nakedly, is to realize that we are not in control.

The point I want to make is that because of the demands of daily life, most people are simply getting by. They do not have the time, or experience the luxury, or even perhaps the necessity, to look more deeply at the structures we are residing within: those ensphering realities that structure the foundational *why* of our lives.

If you've gotten this far, and are at all familiar with my work, you will be aware that I'm not a person who is very good at receiving the world on the terms with which it has been given to me. There is something deep within my nature that refuses to accept things at face value. This makes me, as you might imagine, rather intense.

The reason that I'm drawing all of this out, is because we find ourselves at a moment in history, where the very future of life hangs in the balance. And when I look around, the people who are making the decisions that affect the greatest number of human beings, and therefore the planetary life, I am flatly unimpressed by their qualifications or their humanity. Many of them seem to have hearts of solid ice. Shitheads seemingly to the core. Many of them dangerously mentally ill.

I note the degree to which many of them have been unconsciously indoctrinated into a system of thought, a worldview, and a mode of being that originates in profound alienation.

It is the fatherly place within me, the place that feels a level of responsibility to my own child, and to all children, to unveil the nature of the drivers of destruction and distraction that are eating our world. I feel an urgent need to throw back the curtain.

If you're able to look out beyond the edge of your own coffee cup, with stability, you begin to recognize that the way that the world is structured, and the way that people are acting, are actually profoundly antithetical to their own interests, and well-being.

This seems paradoxical until you are able to understand the forces that have created the civilization that we find ourselves entangled within.

We moderns are the inheritors of empire. We are the unwitting children of Rome. The civilizational operating system we find ourselves in is not a democracy, no matter what you have been taught in school. The operating system is an empire of domination born out through alienated transactional logic.

It is a self terminating cannibalistic system that eats its young.

Such a system is, by definition, a death cult.

Acculturation into such a system is to become an effective death technician.

This force, a thanatic force, is the underlying field that generates the reality of modernity.

We could call it evil, and it is, but I don't know if that's particularly helpful, because associating this with the demonic obscures its embededness in the mundane, as Hannah Arendt pointed out long ago.

Yet the logic of this death cult, which is as embedded in right angles as it is in immigration policies, structures minds, and worldviews. It has an ethics. Although it is not alive, it has characteristics of a complex adaptive system, and it has an intrinsic urge to perpetuate itself.

My objective here in this volume is straightforward. I'm going to exit you from the death cult.

I don't think you're going to enjoy this very much. But the alternative is that you don't exit the death cult. And since it is a death cult, the endpoint of that is pretty apparent.

Did you know that the etymology of apocalypse is truth revealed?

Welcome to the apocalypse. I'm here to lead you out by taking you through. My qualifications are two: first, I am the grandchild of the witches you could not burn. Second, I've already passed through an apocalypse and got shat out its asshole end. So I assert myself a fairly capable guide. I've already been through hell. It doesn't stick to my fur.

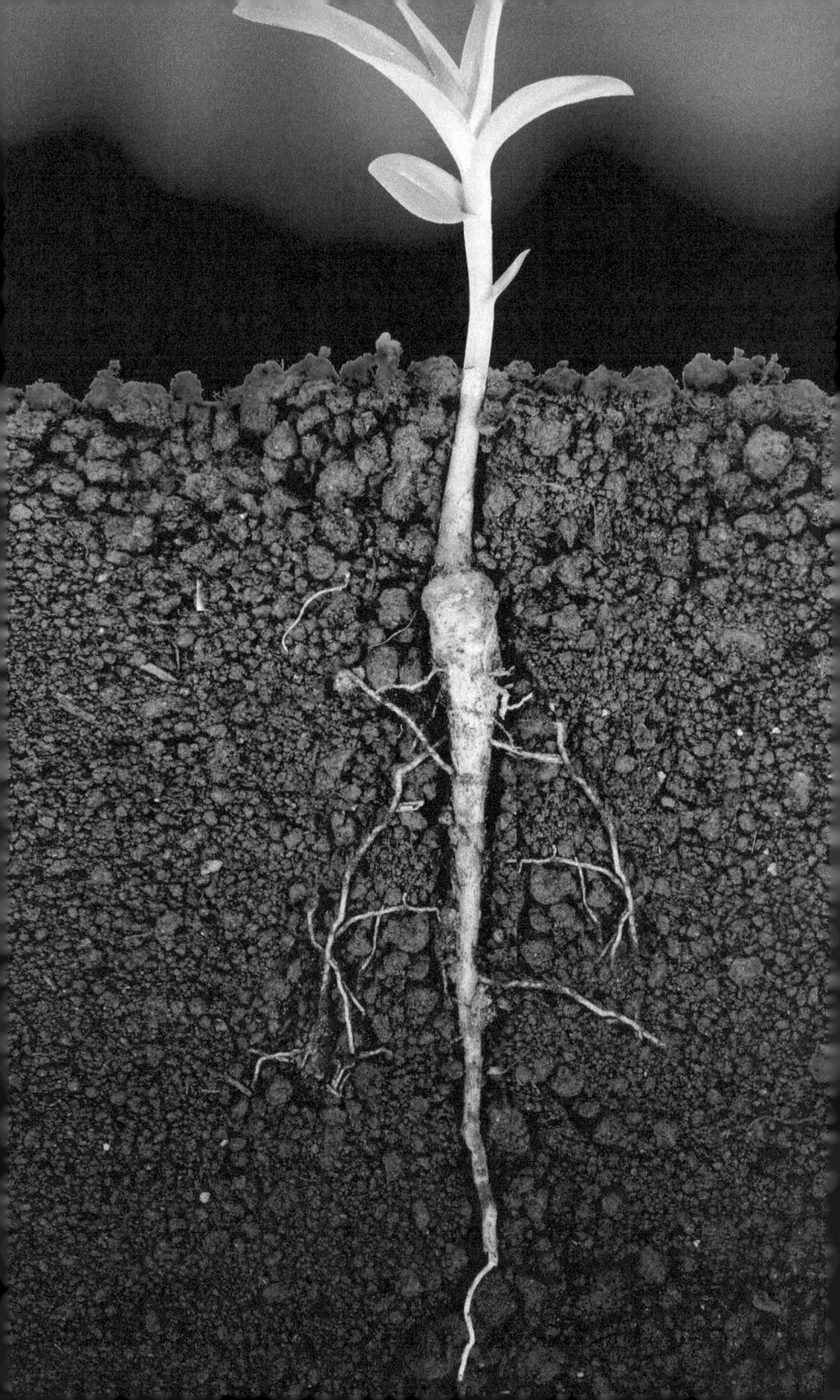

01

# Digging out the Tap-root of Supremacy

⊕

For the past several years, I have been harvesting and planting California Buckeyes during the winter rains. The trees sprout from the buckeye itself, which is about the size of a seven-year-old child's balled-up fist. With the correct amount of rain and sunlight, a taproot breaks out from the body of the nut, extending like a narrow white tail, its knobbly extension dropping straight down. After it has grown several inches, and become convinced it has encountered suitable soil, the trunk of the root birfurcates in a vivid fuchsia split at the edge of the nut, and the tree's first leaves, and what will become its stalk, and later its trunk, unfurl upward from here. Having done this several times now, I learned this year that the seedlings need to be planted in very deep containers. In the first several months of growth, the taproot drops straight down with the same velocity the leaves and stalk rise up. This is different than many other plants, many other trees, which develop broader spreading root systems. Nourished by the hulking nut, the tree's first year of growth is in hyperdrive. If the container holding the Buckeye is too shallow the taproot smashes into its bottom, get frustrated, circles, coils back on itself. It wants to grow straight down. It is seeking the depths.

⊕

When does the modern era begin? What is the dawn of the modern world, the age we know? What are the mental figurations that give rise to it? Humans have been here for at least two hundred thousand years, and yet our recorded history reaches back less than five. Ninety-seven percent of our lineage history is veiled in the shadows of deep time. Yet if we turn toward the origin stories of western civilization, and listen with the ears of trackers, we may yet hear echoes of something older. The stories we have inherited that claim to be 'In the beginning...' aren't nearly ancient enough to be so. Let us pick up the trail, and walk it back, until it dissolves into mist. Possibly, if our senses are sharp enough, our ways of knowing and listening more embodied and nuanced, our sensory radar will penetrate the fog and we will catch a glimpse of the pattern behind the pattern and be able to follow it long after we can see it. I am seeking out the taproot of supremacy. I can see the tree in full form, planted squarely in the psyche of the modern world. I know it came from some seed, some nut: that it grew in us, wasn't always this way.

I assert that we can decolonize the world all we want, but if we don't decolonize people's minds, by which I really mean our hearts, nothing will change. We will simply exchange one set of oppressions for another. From where was it birthed, this taproot of supremacy, and what did it engender? How did things come to be this way? Come, listen in your body with me to the background radiation in the white space behind our origin stories. Let us point our listening at the origin of things.

⊕

Some facts that can be set out:

March 30, 2023: the Vatican formally repudiates the Doctrine of Discovery, 571 years after the papal bull Dum Diversas (1452) authorized Alfonso V of Portugal to reduce any "Saracens (Muslims) and pagans and any other unbelievers" to perpetual enslavement. This papal bull, written nearly six hundred years ago, was one of a trio of authorizations granted by the Vatican to Christian kings that gave the Catholic churches the imprimatur to colonize the non-European (non-Christian) world, and established the legal basis for the enslavement of other people, and the concept of terra nullius (empty lands). When I was in elementary school, a mere forty years ago, I was told that Christopher Columbus discovered America. The papal bull Inter Caetara (1493) explicitly grants to the Christian kings land and title to all lands extending in all directions out from Europe not occupied or governed by Christians.

"And, in order that you may enter upon so great an undertaking with greater readiness and heartiness endowed with the benefit of our apostolic favor, we, [the Vatican] of our own accord, not at your instance nor the request of anyone else in your regard, but of our own sole largess and certain knowledge and out of the fullness of our apostolic power, by the authority of Almighty God conferred upon us in blessed Peter and of the vicarship of Jesus Christ, which we hold on earth, do by tenor of these presents, should any of said islands have been found by your envoys and captains, give, grant, and assign to you and your heirs and successors, kings of Castile and Leon, forever, together with all their dominions, cities, camps, places, and villages, and all rights, jurisdictions, and appurtenances, all islands and mainlands found and to be found, discovered and to be discovered towards the west and south, by drawing and establishing a line from the Arctic pole, namely the north, to the Antarctic pole, namely the south, no matter whether the said mainlands and islands are found and to be found in the direction of India or towards any other quarter, the said line to be distant one hundred leagues towards the west and south from any of the islands

commonly known as the Azores and Cape Verde."
-Inter Caetara (1493)

Upon what premise does it exert this 'moral' authority? Non-christians are not fully human. Here is the signature that we are looking for, the stamp of supremacy. The sanctioned church declares: We christians are human, you pagans are not. Pope Francis names it directly: "Never again can the Christian community allow itself to be infected by the idea that one culture is superior to others, or that it is legitimate to employ ways of coercing others."

I call your attention, here at our beginnings in the present moment to one other place, a photograph in a newspaper article, seemingly unrelated. Here is a white woman in Iowa, in her thirties, who works in a hair salon, speaking about her views of Donald Trump, who has just been indicted. From her own diction, we can infer that she is not highly educated. "There's not enough Republicans supporting him," she says. "He's just very rude. And he doesn't talk like a president is supposed to." I bring your attention to the facial expression. What does supremacy look like?

I am not speaking of white supremacy specifically, because white supremacy is a flavor, a sub-category I would propose to you, of this larger phenomenon of supremacy. Yet supremacy itself, in all its variants, is a form of smugness. A smirk of dismissal. Notice the tilt of the head. The slight uplift of the chin so that she can look down at us. The squint. We are in the realm of archetypes. I mean no disrespect to this particular lady: I am looking through her at the gesture; the place in consciousness from which she addresses us. Now here is the gaze of the man she disdains allegiance for.

Again, notice the gaze, and from where it is directed.

So let us begin with these portraits, the Vatican's repudiation of the Doctrine of Discovery, 571 years after they enshrined it in papal authority, and the smirk of a thirty-something woman in Iowa looking down her nose at us. The act and its expression.

⊕

I remember the first time I ever became conscious of social hierarchy. I was seven years old, and had just been displaced from my home, community, and place. I grew up in a small town in New Hampshire, in the Connecticut river valley. My father was a landscape architect, and at this time my mother did not yet work. We lived in a house that was probably 800 square feet, and several hundred years old. The stairs creaked dutifully every time they were ascended or descended. Downstairs was a kitchen with a screened-in porch, and a living room. Upstairs my parents bedroom, my bedroom, and a single bathroom. Outside the house were other colonial homes like it, 250 years old, and a grid of streets that led up into the forested hills. In five minutes I could be out of the neighborhood and into field and forest. Maybe the town consisted of a thousand inhabitants. There was a central square with a cannon that dated back to the Revolutionary war. A bank, a post office, a couple of restaurants including a greek (for some reason) pizza parlor called Athens Pizzeria. A small, out-of-the way New England town. The kind memorialized now in calendars with glossy photographs of covered bridges at peak autumn foliage. No one we knew had any money. No one I knew. But we were rich in belonging, and I was not aware of class, of status.

⊕

As an exercise in awareness, I like to attempt to reach back into the heartspace and mindview of our earliest human ancestors, to attempt to place myself at the origin of our species in the Kalahari two hundred thousand years ago. Because some of the culture of the Kalahari is still intact, this exercise is not as fanciful as it seems, as we have experiential contact yet with this source culture.

What we think of as alienation, is, functionally, an absence of belonging. In an existence where we belong to the universe, where we are part of it and viscerally experience our relatedness, our kinship, with all there is, we are woven together with all of Life. Through the lens of this sacred unity, nothing is alien, nothing is untethered. Through the ropes of relating we have access to all the information in the universe: in-formation. Information is energy in formation. Within this mode of belonging, there is no need for the kind of God that monotheism proposes, because God is experienced in everything, including us. This experience of belonging is down beneath language, beneath sensation. It is a visceral immersion in *with*.

What moderns call God is an artifact of our alienation. The way we think about the Creator is confused. Something benign yet not human, unfathomable, accessible possibly through altered states, mediated by trained initiates. It supposes that we are somewhere down here, and there is someone up there running things. The hegemony of European rationalism, so called, which rejects as irrational those things that cannot be explained 'scientifically'–and therefore relegates religion to the realm of the antique–misses the point entirely, which is that religion expresses a yearning. It is right there in the etymology of the word. A yearning to be tied back to the creative wellspring, the Source (re-ligio). What we call God–and assuredly our attempts to illustrate this, constrain it in human form, put a beard on it and paint it on a chapel ceiling are much deeper a reflection of the hall of mirrors of our own narcissism than anything approaching reality–arises from the felt intuition that we have been cut off from the wellspring of reality, and long for a relationship with it. The problem is that we've become consumed with what this looks like, and forgotten how it feels.

This yearning for God–and to be crystal clear I heartily endorse as crucial both this yearning, and its consummation–is the yearning to not be alienated, not an orphan of an uncaring universe, but a child of belonging. The yearning for God, its essence, its distillate, is a yearning for belonging, in a cosmic sense. To FEEL part of the divine reality, the divine family, the eternal flux.

I'm driving toward the taproot of Supremacy, and it has brought me here, to this contemplation of the Divine, which is generally clothed in the poor cloth of our own minds, our own gaze, and our own thinking, and has been formalized over millennia into the varied and yet static forms we generally are made aware of by religion. Yet I direct my attention back, further, to tribal wanderings, to the Jews in the desert, ye brethren of mine, ye wandering tribes of Israel. The old testament God, to whom they entrusted worship, the tetragrammaton, is a God to whom they prayed for what? For a good harvest, for peaceful hearts, for a glimpse at the fabric of the real, for harmony in the home and hearth, for blessing. And the common denominator of all these worthy prayers? Belonging.

Jesus has been as intentionally mistranslated as anyone in history. Yet of crucial import to this conversation (I say this based on having studied, through books, the Aramaic language he spoke) is the fact that contrary to both popular conception and to established church doctrine, Jesus did not say, "Pray to me." He said, "Pray as I pray." He was teaching people how to come back into relationship with the Cosmos. How to *feel* kinship. This is not written in some book. Relatedness is not in a text, in a scripture, be it a torah or otherwise.

*"Seek not the law in your scriptures, for the law is life, whereas the scripture is dead. I tell you truly, Moses received not his laws from God in writing, but through the living word. The law is living word of living God to living prophets for living men.*

*In everything that is life is the law written. You find it in the grass, in the tree, in the river, in the mountain, in the birds of heaven, in the fishes of the sea; but seek it chiefly in yourselves. For I tell you truly, all living things are nearer to God than the scripture which is without life.*

*God so made life and all living things that they might by the everlasting word teach the laws of the true God to man. God wrote not the laws in the pages of books, but in your heart and in your spirit. They are in your breath, your blood, your bone; in your flesh, your bowels, your eyes, your ears, and in every little part of your body.*

*They are present in the air, in the water, in the earth, in the plants, in the sunbeams, in the depths and in the heights. They all speak to you that you may understand the tongue and the will of the living God.*

*But you shut your eyes that you may not see, and you shut your ears that you may not hear. I tell you truly, that the scripture is the work of man, but life and all its hosts are the work of our God. Wherefore do you not listen to the words of God which are written in His works? And wherefore do you study the dead scriptures which are the work of the hands of men?"*

-The Essene Gospel of Peace

When then, did we lose this experience of relatedness? When did we stop reading the book of life in the Living World, studying this living law, and why? Somewhere between the Original Fire tended by the Black Mother of Us All, the matrilineal line with the circle of the village organized around it, and the ritualized alienation of modernity, there are a series of denaturing catastrophes. What were they?

⊕

These catastrophes are stories of being cast out. A sequence of tragic exiles. A repetition of removal from kinship: damning blasts of expulsion. First from the garden of relatedness to all (Eden), then from relatedness with our human brothers and sisters.

If we, again, turn our attention back the Bible, that source document of origin stories that are not really so, we find the story of Cain and Abel. This is still early in the book, Chapter Four, just after the story of Adam and Eve. We are one generation after having been cast out of the garden.

Cain, the first born, is a farmer. Abel, second-born, is a shepherd. Each makes a sacrifice to God: Cain of herbs of the field, Abel of a lambling. God in the story accepts Abel's sacrifice, while disdaining Cain's. Cain rises up and kills his brother, is marked, and cast out (again, the second damning blast from this divine trumpet, for his parents have already been cast out once), and forced to wander.

If we apply the same method we have applied in our analysis of Adam and Eve, seeing this as a sort of fractal radioactive ember of some deeper older story that carries yet throughlines and undercurrents of meaning, applying our tracking skills, listening for the pattern of the story beneath the story, we can ask also who wrote this story, and whom did it benefit, and to what end, and perhaps some useful things will come into clearer view out of the mist.

The first alienation is from original belonging, which has been blamed on a woman (the Earth) in partnership with a snake (our Indigeneity). If we unlock this story, and open it, we find that contrary to established meanings, the turn toward belonging is back toward the feminine, and toward contact with the ground (indigenous people are earth-based [chthonic] people).

The second story, the story of Cain and Abel, narrates the entrance of war into the human story. Both children of the original mother, brother turns against brother. This is a story of the generation of tribal [civilizational] lines. It is attempting to explain a diaspora in the human family as a result of murder. Again, let us take as accurate the essence of its effect, as we have taken as accurate the essence of the effect of the story of Adam and Eve. Through the story of Adam and Eve, we arrive in medias res, in the middle of the play, as it were, in a world where people are alienated from Nature. The story is attempting to tell us how things got to be this way. So too, in the story of Cain and Abel, we arrive in a world of diverse civilizations in diverse places, with different skins, where brother murders brother. People are alienated from other people. The children of the original mother no longer know they are of the same family. Crumbsnatchers from the original fireplace scattered to the wind.(1) Some of them are farming peoples, tied to place. Some of them are herding peoples, nomadic. They have lost the remembrance of their shared roots, their common origin, their shared mother, the common hearth.

What is missing from either of these forms are the original peoples, the hunter gatherers, so we know that this is a story whose origin is within the past 12,000 years. A story situated after the birth of agriculture. By the time Cain and Abel happens, the diaspora from the Kalahari is a fact lost already to ancient history, beyond the pale of the backcast gaze, forgotten. Civilizations in this next era have organized themselves around two principles: that of tilling the soil, and that of herding animals. Tilling cultures, which are anchored to place, have become more urban, and seats therefore of technology. The etymology of the word Cain, in Aramaic (kain), links it to 'forge' or 'smith'. Cain is a farmer, but also a metal worker: a skilled artisan, a city-dweller. Cain's sacrifice is rejected, and he kills Abel. In the story he does this with a rock, but I find myself wondering about this. Here is a smith, a bronze-age artisan, killing a shepherd. I find it hard to believe he would not have done so with a weapon forged by his own hand.

It is my intuition that with the same forge that bronze-age humans have shaped the plow, they shaped also the sword. We have come into the era of intensified fire, the era of the forge, and with this ability to liquify and shape metal we have figured out how to smith tools that will break open the earth and break open bodies. We can shatter stone and bone, now. We have crossed a technical threshold of intrusion.

This technical wherewithal has been harnessed to tilling the soil, as well as to defending the city. This culture has begun to stockpile grain, to reserve it against the coming of winter, against the possibility of drought or flood. We guard against famine. In the movement that precedes this, thousands of years before, the movement that gives birth to settled agriculture, there is the transition from hunter gatherer lifestyles–utterly dependent on the Living World–to planting.

Let us view this as a continuum. Someone, we can imagine, realizes that the fruit they eat has seeds, begins to understand that from these seeds grow new plants, and with them more fruit. It is not difficult to imagine an interim phase, a phase where our ancestors were hunting and gathering, yet also planting along the migration routes. We were following the animals, moving with them in cycles. Why not enrich the routes with the seeds of the plants we wish to harvest? Would there have been some kind of interdiction in this? Would this have felt like a violation of the original pattern? Disrespect to some form of belonging?

I don't see how. I can imagine the original peoples traveling–

and this is in deeptime yet– let us say a hundred thousand years ago, through landscapes, savannah, with features that change, annually, and yet slowly so. I can imagine the animals stopping to drink at a lake here, a watering hole. I can imagine my uber-grandparents pausing by the water to drink, I can imagine them planting some of the seeds they had gathered a little distance off from the water's edge, and telling their children. I imagine those same children, some generation later, harvesting fruit from these trees as they too follow the animals.

In order for this to happen–the psychic innovation of altering the landscape–shaping it to better provision them, something has already happened in the consciousness of the human. Some agency being birthed. Something like Will. Some impulse of gardening.

We are, at this time in history, one hundred thousand years ago, all trackers. Our sensory capabilities are so far beyond present-day imagining as to be almost unfathomable. We possess possibly not quite our current level of finger-level dexterity, for our hands then were likely not spending much time writing, scrolling, playing piano, tapping on keys. But the body, in general, would have been fit–packed dense with muscle, and agile–at a level hardly imaginable to anyone but the most extremely elite athletes. This physicality, developed through the everyday necessity of migrating, through the sheer physicality of surviving, is paired with an agility that again we would find remarkable. The quickness of hand, the quickness of mind of the hunter. These are people with no stress whatsoever in our contemporary definition of it. There are no deadlines, no bills to pay, no jobs, no bosses. The economy doesn't expand and contract. We are all part of the ancestral village: no one struggles with isolation, there are no single mothers, no one doing it on their own. In this absence of stress, the people are ventral: their connection systems are online all of the time. Their ability therefore, the performance of these humans, their neurobiological fluidity, is off the charts.

Animals are psychic. Did you know that? They can read your thoughts. And so the people are expert, also, in veiling their minds, quieting them down to nothing. They reside in a continual present, masters of what we would call mindfulness all. And their attention flows through the senses synaesthetically.

They are barefoot, always, with feet that read the laylines of energy in the earth, feet that aid in navigation. Hands and skin that reading the meaning, scent, and humidity of wind. Hands that sense for energy, sense for tracks, sense for water like dowsing wands. Radar hands. Beings reading, through their profound embodiment, the energy landscape just barely veiled by matter. I would propose to you that at this time in our evolutionary history, the hegemony of visuality was not yet in place. People did not primarily see the world. The conscience was not, as Richard Sennet would later assert, of the eye. The refinement of senses was oriented into the felt. We were using the original intelligences with which the human organism is so richly endowed, which arises when the autonomic physiology is stabilized in its baseline state of social engagement. We possessed, at this time, original integrated sensing. We felt everything. And within this feeling, we are people who speak bird language, people who have built ropes with all of the Creation, inhabiting a landscape humming with meaning, with conversation, where we, at will, can pick up and try on the minds of the animals, step into the mind of the cheetah, possibly see through his eyes. Energy beings feeling our way through the pattern language of the Living World.

We, part of the fabric of unity, step through the doorways of individual identity and across the chain of being, becoming the rocks, the sun-baked mud, wearing the mind of the acacia trees, the impala. These uber-grandparents of us all, sensorily and bodily awake in a manner that exceeds our definitions of alertness and embodiment, connected to everything, reading the great book of nature. These are our parent's parents, all of us.

Some, we can imagine, over the spans of deep-time, might have a proclivity to walk less. Might have more stationary attitudes, might have been more meditatively inclined. Might have wanted to sit in one spot. Might have elected, or been asked to stay in one place and tend to the trees. Might have been injured and needed to rest. There are many reasons, perhaps, why some might not have been able, or inclined, to migrate. Perhaps the passing groups bring them food. Perhaps those who stay those ancient winters starve to death, and their skeletons, picked clean by carrion, are encountered the following spring on a reverse migration and revered. Under the first orchards I imagine the bones of some of these early ancestors who could not accumulate enough calories in certain seasons to make it across. I can imagine the bones draped with flowers picked by the tribe wandering past.

A failed crop and the early farmers fall. An early stationary village winks out, like the last ember of a fire.

Is this why God is not pleased with Cain? Because Cain's way of life, at its beginnings, is tenuous?

Abel, the shepherd...Is Abel the original tribe, the hunter gatherer ancestry, murdered? Is this what the story means? Who wrote this story?

From this same ancestral line are there people who, rather than continually following the animals–how much work it is!– capture some rather than kill them and then begin to travel with those? Would these have been sheep? I doubt it, though I don't know. Some kind of four-legged that could have been eaten. Someone suggests, it seems inevitable in hindsight...we're walking our entire lives, following the herd. Let's keep the herd with us.

I can imagine, once again, early experiments. How do you keep the herd near you? Do you hobble some animals? Choose an animal that cannot run away? Looking back into these mists of deep time I wonder. At some point, there are people with herds. I don't know if they are stationary. I doubt it. The animals follow the available food, accompanied by humans or no.

Abel is from this lineage. These lines, both of them, Cain and Abel, have opted for easier lives. Acquired some form of food insurance. Have opted to not depend utterly on Nature, and by the time of their story I believe that both of them have already put on supremacy mind and are having trouble taking it off. In what particular sense?

There is a kind of profound humility that comes when you depend entirely upon Nature for your survival. It is co-extant with the bone-deep knowledge of starvation. We moderns, consumers of empty calories, of Cheetos and Coca-cola, have lost contact with this, but our ancestors were experts in deprivation. We know, we knew what it meant to starve. Some of us still know.

Our small band hunter gatherer ancestors did not have refrigerators, storehouses, walls to keep out marauding others be they animal or human.

There is a kind of profound humility that comes from the daily forced reminder that being alive is a gift, and that this gift can be withheld. Nature has no bankruptcy protection: doesn't make loans. Go negative with calories for long enough and you will die. There are no government bailouts for biology.

Both emerging lines, that of the farmer, and that of the shepherd, seem to me like bets to try to change the odds, to try to sweeten the deal. Insurance against hardship.

Here, in Cain and Abel, is a story we have turned into an inverted kaleidoscope, an attempt to see through jumbled patterns and construct an instrument to look backwards into deep time.

⊕

By virtue of this insurance do we necessarily step in the direction of supremacy? Is it possible to have some form of abundance and not accumulate the gain and accrue it to ourselves? Not come to the conclusion that we are somehow better than those who do not have?

More intelligent? Closer to God? More blessed? Do we not tell stories that confirm us in our biases? Happy is the one who does not attribute success to himself, but rather increases their gratitude. How many 'successful' and I put the word in quotes, as I interrogate it here...how many successful modern people do you know who will look you in the eye if you ask them about their flourishing and tell you it was luck? Most of the people I know attribute it to their own talents. Even born on third base, when they score they narrate stories about hitting home runs.

Is this the origin of supremacy? A shift in the manner of living, civilizations ago, that took us out of direct contact with the necessity of the now? Out of being provided for by a benevolent universe? The first hedging of bets, the first accumulation, and then a need, retrospectively, to explain why we had food and someone else did not? To story this in a hierarchy and declare that one mode of living was more pleasing to God?

⊕

And yet I cannot help but feel, because I observe it in myself, that the taproot of supremacy is feeling alone. It comes from feeling abandoned by everything. Feeling abandoned, feeling cast out, we reserve some little part of the psyche of universe and call it *self*. We withdraw from relationship, and this contraction is ego.

I know something about this. My own seven-year-old self's balled-up fist. The root of supremacy breaks out from the fist, dropping straight down, this white tail. The bifurcation, the splitting that gives rise to the tree, is its mirror image extending in the opposite direction. The moment that we feel more-than, the moment supremacy takes hold, it births an anti-self. Inferiority. And from the sacred unity we split into this bivalent structure of better-than, worse-than. More-than, less-than. Suddenly there is hierarchy everywhere. We are above, and we are below. A hall of mirrors, a world of ranked selves. We are in exile. Cast out.

I pick up with another origin story here, this one Greek. The Odyssey of Homer. The great Odysseus, that man skilled in all ways of contending, is marooned far from home, far from his native land, his steadfast wife, his beloved son. Taken for dead by the people, his hall has been over-run by suitors, whom his wife forestalls by weaving a tapestry, claiming that when it is finished she will marry one of them. Each night by candlelight she unweaves it, pulling the warp and weft apart. The governing yearning of this text is *nostos*, the Greek word that means longing for home.

We are a handful of millennia back now, three or so, by the time The Odyssey is authored. In this story, incandescent at its center, illuminating the entire arc of action, is this longing to come home.

At its inception modernity is already in exile upon exile. Cast out from home and hearth. No longer gathered around the original fire.

⊕

I didn't become conscious of social hierarchy until I had been taken from my people and from my place. At seven years old my family moves away from the small town where my sense of kinship to everything flourished. I experience this as a kind of kidnapping, of being abducted by those people who were supposed to take care of me. It shatters my trust in my parents. I have not been able to trust them again. I go with them willingly at the time because I don't understand that we are leaving. Have you ever loved something so much that you didn't realize it could be taken away from you?

This is my own private experience of being cast out. As an outcast I become suddenly conscious of hierarchies. Of the status valence of different clothing brands, different kinds of cars. Alienated, I suddenly adorn myself in symbols of worth, and I hierarchize others. Polo is better than Izod is better than JC Penny. Ferrari is better than Mercedes is better than Toyota is better than Ford. White is better than Asian is better than Indian is better than Black. The world becomes a ranking system. I only realize this because I no longer belong. My focus shifts from the feeling of kinship to the gaze of exile.

⊕

There is a concept in biology that says ontogency recapitulates phylogeny. It means that the development of an individual organism expresses the evolutionary history of its entire lineage. Look at the development of a human embryo in utero, and you can see it passing through phases that resemble a lizard, a chicken, a monkey: all of our evolutionary forebears, before it starts to differentiate itself into something unmistakably human. Elements of the theory have been disproved, but the notion of this, the fractality, it holds up. Does the arc of an individual life also recapitulate the arc of cultural ancestry?

I know what it means to be cast out and not know why. The body wants to–needs to, perhaps–make up a story. Why were we thrown out of the garden? Who writes the story? The priestly class? Let's blame it on the woman and the snake. My own grapplings with this give rise to supremacy.

Impotent in the face of what happened, unable to change it, unable to bear it, the grief too radioactive to name, the loss too white-hot to know, to feel, I cordon it off in parts of my psyche that are unreachable and the deepest most vital parts of my kinship with everything freeze. I become ice. Deeply deeply alone. Turning this alienation over and over in my mind, like a stone, I come to the conclusion that I am better-than. But as always with this formulation, its twin is also true. I come to the conclusion that I am worse-than as well, only this I refuse to know.

Thirty seven years it takes me to make my way home, back to this original self. My path there is circuitous, and it passes, in 2012, through psychiatric hospitalization when my mind cleaves around this birfucated root. As a result of childhood trauma I had become someone with two acceleratingly opposed experiences of self: one seeking confirmation that I was superior, its manifestation in accumulating evidence of my own perfection. Things that provided evidence of specialness I adhered to this sense of self. Certain accomplishments. Degrees from elite institutions. Bulletpoints on a résumé. Things that contradicted it, and there were many, I refused to know, because I didn't have a structure of self that could accommodate them. If I was superior, then failure couldn't be part of me. And so if I failed there was then something wrong with the contest–I had to disqualify it. The parts of myself that felt grief, loss, absence, doubt, weakness...experiences of which I was ashamed, felt guilty, was embarrassed, or defeated–none of these had a place to live. They hovered, anchorless, tired birds with no place to roost on the tree of my superiority.

Ironically, neither of these stances–the stance looking down at, or the stance looking up at–have anything to do with relating. With feeling kinship. Remember the woman in Iowa? We are in the domain of the hegemony of the eye. What is striking in her portrait is the gaze, and the place in consciousness it is coming from. The head is tilted off to the side and she is looking down at. Not at us only, but at everything. Off to the side of the world, she looks down at it, at something beneath her. Something outside of her, unrelated. But what is beneath–the everything of it all–looks back at her and in moments of vertigo, of inversion, it is her beneath, looking up. The stance engenders its own opposite.

In my own life, in 2012, a series of increasingly stressful events took place that included the death of my grandmother, my parents moving toward divorce, me losing my job, and my wife leaving our spiritual community. I watched things break apart like a series of dominoes falling in slow motion. My ancestry, my family of origin, my livelihood, my community. Consumed by anxiety, I stopped being able to calm my autonomic nervous system, and I stopped being able to sleep. An internal edifice collapsed– I can remember it happening. It was as if all the things that were holding me together, all of the structures built on the stability of other people and parts of my identity, shook down in an earthquake. I didn't sleep for forty days, until I had completely lost control of my own mind. And what was revealed, plain as day when I could no longer in any way steer my own thoughts, was that I had cleaved in two. A taproot of supremacy, and a tree of inferiority. Everything went upside-down.

Supremacy is always schizophrenic. That's part of what I am here to tell you, possibly the point of this essay. There is no such thing as superiority. It is always superiority and inferiority conjoined. They are coupled. The taproot and the tree it nourishes. The above and the below. It is always bi-valent, this forgetting. This is not something I read in a book somewhere. This is something I lived through.

I was plunged down into all of the parts of myself I had been unable to metabolize at all. A plunge beneath the surface, replete with terror. A hell realm.

But–and I feel that this is important to emphasize–while that place is real, as real as its ethereal opposite–what gives rise to it, the roadway that connects it to here, to this earthly plane, is this split structure of supremacy.

The evangelical fervor around sin, the pulpit hectoring about hell-fires and damnation, is a possible place to get sent only because, earlier in the sermon, the christians thought themselves to be superior; convinced themselves that heaven was their due. Thus the current pope's warning: Never again can the Christian community allow itself to be infected by the idea that one culture is superior to others... And yet. And yet- nearly all of the christian communities I've ever encountered do.

We think we are superior because we have been cast out. All of us. The entire lot.

We live in a supremacy engine. It is the fuel of this suicidal/genocidal cult of death worship that passes for a culture.

And yet, neither superiority, or its anti-self, its twin of inferiority has anything to do with relationship. Both are contractions, balled-up fists, to avoid the pain of relating. Of how deeply uncomfortable it is to have contact–felt contact–with Self or Other. How much it fucking hurts to touch and to be touched. How much it fucking hurts.

Whether we are above or below someone else doesn't matter. The point is that, in either case, we are not with. Neither one knows anything about kinship.

⊕

We are not superior to anything. But neither are we inferior. We cannot be either, for we are made of the same stuff as everything else.

I had to rebuild my mind. It took me six years. I would never wish the experience on anyone, yet neither would I trade it for anything. I was afforded the opportunity to perform an archeology of shadows, and what I excavated was not merely mine.

Yes, I had attached to it, and had made it my own, but much of it was inherited.

The reclamation of original self is something that we should probably all undertake. I remember the moment when my child-self came back online. I had gone to extreme measures to retrieve him. I've drunk ayahuasca hundreds of times, passed through the insane asylum, got spat out the backside of hell to rescue and resuscitate my original indigenous self.

I've written about this elsewhere. When I re-united with him, after thirty-seven years, it was about 5:30 in the morning and I was lying on the forest floor. I had just moved back to ten acres of pristine forest and was able, for the first time since being cast out of the forest of my childhood mind, to feel the grief of it without drowning– because I had returned to the forest.

I had been meditating on a cushion at the moment this happened, sitting before dawn in a circle of Douglas Fir trees, but when the grief came it enveloped me in a cloak as black as death and I couldn't hold my body up and I collapsed. The air itself became funereal.

I had met this child self before, in ceremonies, accompanied him back into vitality slowly, quietly, with simple presence over many years.

But when he came back to me it was thermonuclear: there was nothing subtle about it.

From the deepest well of blackness, smothering in grief I crossed an internal threshold back into rage. A polyvagal threshold. My body tensed as through encased in steel bands, and I felt a scream begin to organize beneath my body. I stood up.

It came up through me, slowly, yet whitehot, rising through my feet, into my calves, then my knees, my thighs, my hips. My throat began to organize as it moved up through my torso and I found myself gulping air, like some kind of fish.

When I screamed it knocked the roof off the valley.

A silence ensued, and then a cacophony of barking dogs followed.

⊕

I write to understand what I know. I write to allow it to come through me. I don't know what I am going to say when I start out. It is improvisational. I begin with an intuition, and I walk in the lineage of trackers. I follow trails to see where they will go, and I let my heart guide me.

Three quarters of the way through writing this essay, out working on the land where I am building a cabin, the land where I have recovered my original self, I step on a rusty nail. I step on it at the precise moment when I say out loud something deeply uncaring about my neighbor there, who clothes himself in all the garments of being an asshole, but nevermind that. I harvest a rusty nail, deservedly so for my rantings when I claim to be focused on unity and healing. I feel it drive up squarely through the sole of my shoe and into my foot. The universe has bitten me at the instant of my hypocrisy. Serves me right.

I hobble off, get in the car, call for medical attention, trying to remember the last time I received a tetanus shot. Two nurses assure me I can wait until the following morning to come in: it is around dinner time. I return home, wash out the wound, lay down.

In bed, horizontal, my immune system begins to have a reaction. I feel the lymph nodes in my groin activate, then those under my chin. My face tightens involuntarily, then my jaw, my teeth grind. My neck begins to writhe. My heart feels a specific kind of pain that it unfamiliar to me. Realizing I will not sleep easily, I drive myself to the Emergency Room.

They see me pretty quickly, and congratulate me for coming in. It isn't primarily tetanus they are concerned about, but a bacterial infection from the puncture. They put me on two simultaneous courses of antibiotics and send me home. The moon is totally full this night, and I stand and gaze upon her for some minutes as I'm getting into my car. It is about one am, and there is a lagoon across from the hospital, in which some variant of waterbird is screeching, keeping all of the animals awake if any of them can sleep in the great brightness. The sky is cloudless, it is the beginning of spring. The moon's radiance is vast and quiet. Her power like a slow magnet, drawing the listening of the land upward.

I drive home, climb into bed. Are you ok? my wife asks. I assert that I am, then do not sleep all night. The next day I continue working on the cabin, stopping to prop my foot up at intervals. It is nearly finished, and I continue to hustle. In mid-afternoon I return home. I eat dinner with my family, go to bed early, but for the second night I lie there, not sleeping. This doesn't cause me distress, not really– I've endured forty nights without sleep, a few don't really bother me– but it is not comfortable. Sometime after midnight I decide that if I'm not going to sleep I'd rather do it at the cabin in the forest. I rise, dress, leave the house quietly. This night is cloudy, and the air is heavy, and still, as if nature herself is holding her breath. I drive with the windows down, and the entire ride there is this weight, this expectancy, in the air.

I arrive in the forest, walk out onto the land, make my way to the cabin. The moment I arrive it begins to rain. Softly at first, just a sort of mist, and then gathering momentum.

I've built the cabin with a clear roof so that you can see the sky, and I lie there, in bed, listening to rain plink onto the polycarbonate roof. The forest exhales scents of spring, there is a slight wind, and with the rain the sense of waiting begins to dissipate, the held breath begins to move. I lie there, feeling myself from the inside, feeling my breath. I think back to the original fire, and it occurs to me that these ancestors whose minds I am trying to put on, living several hundred thousand years ago, were naked. They did not wear pajamas. I strip down, underneath the blankets, and lie there, shivering vividly, feeling the energy course through my body, the way the sudden coldness of the mattress beneath gives my backside an edge.

All night it is like this, a second night, I never fall over the cliff into sleep, but toss, turn, shivering. I curl up in a foetal position on my side to get warm. My mind is quiet, mostly, there is the sound of the rain knocking on the roof, the movement of air. At some point I open my eyes and it is light out. I am neither tired nor rested.

That was yesterday. For most of the day I work, and then early last night I head to bed. I take a bath in epsom salts, a swig of magnesium and melatonin and valerian, and fall into bed at 7:30. I fall into a deeper sleep. At some point in the night I awaken and my wife is lying next to me, reading. I touch her side, rest a finger against the bare skin above the crease of her hip, and fall back asleep.

In my dream I am trying to reach my mother, who is dying. She is with my father, with whom I have not spoken in three years. I am trying, in the dream, to get to her, but it is one of those dreams in the genre of being unable to run, where I cannot, despite my best efforts, cause this to happen. I cannot get to her. I am in some unnamed city late at night. There are dark hills covered with dark buildings, empty roadways in an urban grid. My cellphone, on which I am trying to call her, has an unfamiliar screen where the telephone typepad should be and I cannot dial out. Some browser window will not close. I cannot fix it. When the phone rings–and I know it is them calling– I cannot answer it.

Strangely, and I only put this together now, writing these words, the final scene in the dream, where I cannot pick up the phone, happens with me standing next to a church building of some kind where (a priest?) (a Jesuit?) someone in priestly vestments is sitting in a small office documenting something. In the dream it is the middle of the night, and he sits there with the door open, in a pool of light against the greater darkness while I have a faint sense that I am disturbing him. It doesn't occur to me to ask him for help. He is mentally elsewhere I sense.

Just before I awaken I take the phone and smash it. I am lost somewhere in the city. Some old jacketed religious figure is jotting in a book. The last thing I remember before waking is breaking it, the screen of the phone shattering.

I awaken and lie there, in bed. It occurs to me that I have blamed my parents since I was seven years old, and that I have stuck to this story, built a pretty grand edifice of narrative identity around it.

Suddenly, and I cannot unsee this, I realize that my attachment to this view of that string of events–them deciding, with two small children, that they must leave the tiny New England town they had moved to and return to St. Louis, where their families are from–my attachment to seeing this only through my own experience of loss, is, in fact, a remnant of supremacy.

It is not the only way to understand those events. I realize, suddenly, that what fixes that interpretation as the only possible one is my not feeling ok. That if I am ok, and I am, that what happened is also ok. That as painful as it was, it set the necessary trajectory for my life, and that even though it hurt, even though it still hurts, my ability to be sitting here writing these words, to have embarked upon my career, taken on the work I do in the world, all of it hearkens back to that.

None of this realization is cognitive; very little of it comes through thought. It is something I feel first, know in my body. It gives me pause. I find that I am no longer particularly tired, and I get up. I come downstairs, and make tea. It turns out to be shortly after 2:30 am.

I sit down on the couch at a certain point, where I am now, writing these words.

I will probably always be sexist, racist, classist. I forget myself and fall back into supremacy mind, but I know what it is now. It is the defining mental illness of modernity. The taproot of supremacy is feeling alone. I hold, lightly at this moment, my family of origin, many of whom I have pushed away. I am yet, despite all my work in connection, in the habit of feeling alone. I am yet, in moments of difficulty, prone to isolation. Two-and-a-half years of COVID. A world in polycrisis. The everyday difficulties of marriage, family, raising a teenager. How much it actually hurts to be in contact. I still know so much about feeling alone.

I suppose this is why I think of supremacy as a taproot. The single penetrating illness of separation. The head turned slightly to the side, looking askance at a world that we cannot or will not feel. A world that we have to set over there–elsewhere–because it is too painful. Because the contact of kinship, when we have it, hurts almost as much as its lack. If I'm honest, and I stand in the perspective of my family, looking back at me, I can see in myself the Trumpian gaze that I abhor.

This is the root I am still digging it out. That reflex of turning away. Perhaps I will always be digging it out.

## 02

# On Annihilation

⊕

Let's start with a poem.

### THE NIKE OF SAMOTHRACE

I exist where the wave meets the Ocean.
Where deepest yearning meets identity.
Where everything you've ever been in this Life
And all the songlines you've tread before,
Unite in the feeling of this present moment.

It is 4 am and rain beats down on the roof.
Somewhere a cat sleeps, sphinx-like.
The conquerors, when they came, cut off the heads and noses of the
 great statues
Because those who made them were animists,
And knew the God could come into the stone.

Those who built this world began by beheading the last.
They cut the nose off the Sphinx so she could not breathe.
Deprived of breath, the God withers they believed.

But is it so?
And who is deprived of breath?
COVID comes, taking our breath.
A knee on the neck of George Floyd-
Taking the breath.
Chainsaws in the Amazon, taking the breath.
The conquerors of this modern world
came, extinguishing the breath-
But of whom?

I contemplate the Nike of Samothrace,
Winged Victory,
Headless in the Louvre.
Plundered by a Frenchman from a rubble pile in the Aegean.
Placed on a pedestal,
Fetishized like an animal taxidermied in a zoo.
The statue has no head.

And yet Winged Victory does.
Painstakingly,
And painfully as well,
I grow her a new head, in my mind's eye.
And yet, through the transmutation of Unity
Find that it is, in fact, myself who is growing a new head.

All heads are born from hearts
This is the neuro-embryonic way.
A drumbeat in your ears lays down neural wiring
Firing
In Cascades
Lacelines of meaning
Sonic signatures of rememberance.

Remembrance.
That was dis-membered
By history
By greed
By war
Conquest
Power over.

Singing sung lucid dreamed
Back into vividness.

From the stump of a neck
Veins, sinew, animated by Spirit
By requirement to know itself,
Re-assembling
Like councils long disbanded
Re-aligning
Like songlines paved over
Re-constituting
Like alliances governed
By a shared vision of peace.

From my heart flows upward
My head coming together.
Deep within its center the memories
Of everything that ever was.

A listening that drops to the furnace
At the center of the Earth &
Rises to the shaking of the Stars

It is all alive
Humming with mystery

Vision opening

The ability to see,
The ability to see through
Piercing
Penetrating
The veils that would obscure us from what simply is.

A wreath around her head,
For she was wearing one
Isn't simply a wreath.

These leaves twisted by Divine hands
Into a crown, an amulet, a bower are in fact
Her antennae.

Sensory apparatuses—
Conveying the living pattern intelligence.
Clairvoyance.
Clairaudience.
Clairsentience.
Synaesthesia.

How words fall short, all of them.

I bow to the Nike of Somathrace,
Winged Victory.
Beheaded by Rome,
Which fell once
And whose imprint is falling again.

Arises here, now,
The opportunity to find the place
In the center of the center of the center
Where the wave meets the Ocean—

For that is who we are.

In 168 BC, at the Battle of Pydna, during what would become known as the Third Macedonian War, the Roman legions, in flexible formation, moving over uneven ground, defeated the Macedonian phalanx, a more traditional war formation, ultimately routing the Macedonians, and sending their leader fleeing. The leader, Perseus of Macedonia, was later captured from an island in the Aegean (Samothraki), where he had sought refuge in a temple (The Temple of the Greater Gods), which was under the guardianship of a Winged Goddess. He was taken to Rome, paraded through the streets manacled, then expurgated to an underground dungeon in Alba Fucens in central Italy, where the Romans, who didn't believe in the Macedonian gods, but didn't disbelieve in them altogether, and were aware that Perseus was likely under the protection of forces they did not understand, demurred from killing him outright, yet did so eventually by depriving him of sleep, or so we are told.

The statue of the Winged Goddess was beheaded, as the Romans sought not merely to kill their enemies, but to kill the Divinities of their enemies. The Romans sought to kill people, but what they wanted to extinguish was a worldview, and worldviews are bound up in our comprehension of the Divine. Knowing that the Macedonians were animists, aware that the Goddess might come into the stone through the breath, they removed her head. I find myself wondering if this was done ceremonially. Beheaded, and plundered from the Temple of which she was guardian, she might have been lost to history, except that she is not. You can visit her in the Louvre, where she is known as the Nike of Samothrace.

Deprived of her gaze, her listening, her voice, it is hard for me to yet gender the statue female, though she undoubtedly is. Yet gaze upon her beauty. Gaze upon the sculpture, made of stone, the garments of which are rendered shear– and marvel at being able to see, somehow, her skin, as it were, through the fabric of the gown blown by the winds, knowing that she is in fact made of stone, and made several thousand years ago. The artistry!

It is, you will observe, a rather macabre statue at this point. I wonder what it says about us moderns, and our lack of sensitivity to the energies in objects, that we don't seem to notice this? The contrast between the regal beauty of the body and the absence of a head, which makes this notional aliveness a deeply vacated proposition, is not lost on anyone who understands that she did, at one time, have a head. Imagine how beautiful and sovereign she must have been before she was beheaded by the Romans. If the artist could render the stone garments transparent, imagine her gaze. But we are accustomed to statues without heads. We have seen Roman, Greek, and Egyptian statuary all deprived of limbs and heads. It seems normal to us. Its meaning fails to register.

The Roman Empire was, to my knowledge, nearly unmatched in its annihilatory glee. The Romans had a pure zeal for war engines, delighted in combat. They were whole-heartedly obsessed with what the Irish poet John O'Donohue refers to as our 'fatal attraction to aggression.' If we explore theories of war, which have been catalogued and outlined with precision since at least the time when Sun-Tzu authored the manifesto that is known to us as *The Art of War*, we can find two broad camps arrayed in terms of their understanding of what war is, and these camps are distinguished principally by whether or not the civilizations holding the beliefs are under the impression that Nature is above them, i.e., they are part of (or subservient to Nature) and Nature is superior, or whether they are superior to Nature, and Nature is subservient to them.

---

The picture on the following page is a painting of the Nike. It came through in a transmission so intense I had almost no idea what I was painting. I knew it was her, because I could feel her, and I know who she is. But the way that the lines were coming, the paint? Not me. When you look at the painting, relax your eyes. Let them cross. Then you might catch a glimpse of her, if you ask her nicely.

In my explanation here, I am referring explicitly to a body of teaching that I received from my friend & mentor Pete Jackson, an artist of reknown, and a soldier for peace. Pete is a master of the Afro-Brasilian martial art of Capoeira, and a profound student of the martial lineages. In my early years of friendship with him, I was confounded by his contention that the martial arts were a route to peace, until I began to understand what was required to master one's rage.

When a civilization is not alienated from the Source, and understands that culture is subservient to Life, with a capital L, war is understood to be a necessity at times, but it doesn't not trump life. Civilizations with this view tend to precisely structure the rules of war, such that it accomplishes its objectives of dispute resolution, either vis-a-viz territory, dynastic succession, or conflict resolution, within prescribed limits. Pete taught me, for example, about warfare between African tribes where, when war was entered into, the warriors of the opposing tribes would line up, at several hundred yards distance, in parallel. In orderly fashion, moving down the line, a warrior from each side would hurl a spear at the warriors from the other side, until one was struck and killed. When the first warrior was killed, the opposing side was declared the victor. To necessarily complicate matters somewhat, the warrior who killed the warrior from the other side became responsible for the care of the dead warrior's family. This was war that made use of the martial and sovereign energies of self-protection, yet contained them. It recognized war, even killing, as a necessary part of life, but it held constraints upon it. War did not become total.

The fight response, activated hereby, aflame already, and in need of being mastered, was not fanned. No one poured gasoline on the rage.

This manner of war, in civilizations that understand themselves to be part of Nature, is in contrast to war practiced by civilizations that understand themselves to be superior to Nature. The Romans, believing that they were superior to Nature, elided all mention of the Earthly mother from the doctrine of Christianity when it became the official religion of state, which happened in 313 AD, when the Emperor Constantine issued the Edict of

Milan, and which would have been no surprise to anyone who had seen how they conducted war. The Romans indulged their annihilatory glee. They exalted in it. When a civilization believes itself to be superior to Nature, it makes total war.

The streak of fear undergirding this total war, I believe, is the notion that if a single child of the 'enemy' so-called were to live, that child might carry in their hearts the seeds of rebellion. To this end, the civilization that believes itself superior to Nature seeks to annihilate all the seeds that might so one day turn. This story becomes the mythic fulcrum on which turn many stories of dynastic succession, war, rebellion, genocide, and attempts thereto.

The body I am wearing is Jewish, ancestrally. I grew up remote from the practice of this faith, with a spirituality I would call nature-based were I describing it now. When I was about nine years old, in St. Louis, Missouri, I visited a synagogue for the first time. It frightened me quite profoundly. I had trouble articulating this at the time, but from the moment I stepped inside, it felt like I was walking into a crypt. It felt cold as death. Decades later, as I would come to understand the multi-generational trauma of the Holocaust, and the way that it lives on in the bodies, hearts, and minds of Jewish people, I would come to understand that the synagogue felt like a crypt because it was the spiritual home of a people who had been through a genocide during the lives of my grandparents. It felt like a crypt because it *was* a crypt. Inside the synagogue I had premonitions and ancestral recollection of the gas chambers and killing fields I did not yet, at nine years of age, have conscious knowledge of.

The greatest tragedy of trauma may not be the trauma itself, but the automaticity of reaction that results therefrom. If we do not heal trauma, it repeats itself. We are drawn toward it, ineluctably, karmically, to rehash and repeat and resolve what we are stuck on. Moths, in orbit around a flame too incandescent with loss to allow us freedom of movement. Tethered in orbit to a dark star.

Perhaps the incandescent loss at the center of our modern civilization so-called is the first war, some 75,000 years ago I am told, though I believe this not. What did it do, this first shedding of our brother's blood? I would propose that it turned us into automatons. Something that, when struck, strikes back. It robbed of us of the freedom of choice.

Why, oh why, do we seem drawn, gravitationally, to the opposite of what will restore us to Life?

It is little known that, at the dawn of the 20th century, there were two Jewish visions of the future. The vision that materialized after World War II, the Zionist vision, was the creation of a Jewish state. What is not well understood, by the general population, is that there was another group in the Jewish diaspora, another political movement that at the turn of the century had become very influential in Eastern Europe, and was known as the Bund. Central to the social democratic politics of the Bund, was the Yiddish notion of *doikayt*, or *hereness*. "The concept of Doikayt (Yiddish: דאָיקייט lit. 'hereness'), was central to the Bundist ideology, expressing its focus on solving the challenges confronting Jews in the country in which they lived, versus the "thereness" of the Zionist movement, which posited the necessity of an independent Jewish polity in its ancestral homeland, i.e., the Land of Israel, to secure Jewish life."

The Bundists pointed out what was factually obvious. The creation of the State of Israel would displace the people (Palestinians) who already lived there. Colonial displacement, of the sort practiced and prosecuted during the long reign of the church-sanctioned European fever dream that laid the colonial foundations of the modern world order, does not engender peace.

When Perseus of Macedonia died, the Antogonid dynasty came to an end. Rome continued its territorial expansion for several centuries, until it too eventually fell. Yet the form of Imperial Christianity that Rome birthed has been more enduring, and continues. More than a thousand years after the fall of Rome, the thoughtforms of Domination that gave rise to the sense of superiority that caused the Romans to believe they were above the laws of Nature found expression in a series of papal bulls, including Dum Diversas, and Romanus Pontifex, which would lay the 'spiritual' (I use this word loosely and in quotes) and legal theories in place for the Doctrine of Discovery, based in Christian Supremacy, that created the 'justification' for enslavement and colonialism that has set the template for the modern world, leading to 500 years of colonial extraction of lives, labor, and land, and undergirds the polycrisis of modernity. The cthonic and earth-based peoples of Europe were again purged, as they had been in Perseus' time, this time in the name of religion, not Empire. The witches were burned.

Domination mind is never satisfied. It is a devouring beast, and it eats its young as well, rest assured. The weight of history is so great right now. It is a burden. Christian Supremacy, Jewish Supremacy, Islamic Supremacy. All of them boil down to Supremacies, all of which boil down to this original deformation of reality, which is the recognition that we are not superior to Nature. This is the form of the original deviation. Christian Supremacy, Jewish Supremacy, Islamic Supremacy, any Supremacy gives birth, in the moment of its creation, to its opposite, which is carried like a dark twin in the formation of the notion, because when we exchange the horizontal plane for the vertical, the energy that lifts something up, through physics, pushes something else down. In the thoughtforms of the Dominator are the thoughtforms of the Dominated. This formulation is always schizophrenic, always tethers us to its dark matter twin, always deprives us of freedom.

⊕

What is annihilated?

The Jews were nearly annihilated, but they were not. We were not. The Macedonian Empire was annihilated. But also it was not. We were not. The witches were annihilated. But we were not. The annihilator and the annihilated become fused in the fire of rage, it seems to me. Fused in the inferno.

How, oh how, do we heal this? By what alchemy of grief and forgiveness? By what alchemy of coming together? By what alchemy of returning to safety?

Do healed ancestors ever rejoice in someone else's suffering? What terror of insignificance in us insists on annihilation? What arrogance in us pretends to stand outside the laws of Nature? What wound in us refuses to be healed? Refuses to grieve?

Hurt people hurt people.

Shake off the fog of war and it is clear that the bombs we are dropping are falling on our own children...that the only thing being annihilated is our connection with the Source.

Why, oh why, are we so self-destructive, so suicidal, so unable to recognize our own reflection in the faces looking back at us? Why, oh why, is it so hard for us to see our original faces, to remember who we are?

Energy is neither created nor destroyed. Why is it so hard for us to master our rage? This is what Pete was saying. We need the martial arts–what they really are– to contain the energies of annihilation so that we don't burn the house down with us in it. This is the place the martial arts have within the maintenance of the house of peace.

FOR PEACE

As the fever of day calms towards twilight
May all that is strained in us come to ease.

We pray for all who suffered violence today,
May an unexpected serenity surprise them.

For those who risk their lives each day for peace,
May their hearts glimpse providence at the heart of history.

That those who make riches from violence and war
Might hear in their dreams the cries of the lost.

That we might see through our fear of each other
A new vision to heal our fatal attraction to aggression.

That those who enjoy the privilege of peace
Might not forget their tormented brothers and sisters.

That the wolf might lie down with the lamb,
That our swords be beaten into ploughshares

And no hurt or harm be done
Anywhere along the holy mountain.

JOHN O'DONOHUE

03

# Inverting the Logic of Enclosure

⊕

Alnoor Ladha and Lynn Murphy propose in Post Capitalist Philanthropy that capitalism is a self-terminating algorithm based on socializing costs to the many while privatizing gains for the few. What does this mean? This lucid equation, which bears all the elegance of a formal mathematical proof, is the algorithm of capitalism. First, it notes that capitalism moves teleologically toward its own termination. This occurs when, functionally, someone owns everything. The end point of capitalism is when all of the commons (e.g., property, resources, labor, ideas, attention) have been enclosed and extracted by someone (namely owners), and their collective benefit has been transferred to those owners (the few). Some would propose that those owners are the rich, or the ultra-rich. I will propose to you that capitalism has already ended, and that we simply have not realized this yet. Elon Musk won capitalism when he acquired Twitter. The game is over. Congrats Elon, someone had to do it. (What you will notice, I hope, dear reader, is that it is not coincidental that in winning capitalism Mr. Musk has become the most narcissistic person in the world. More on that elsewhere.)

Capitalism is an operating system. It is a kind of economic, political, and cultural software, which I will refer to as wetware. It is a soft overlay on human neurobiology. (Thus wet.) The source code of this operating system is an extraction codex. To operate successfully in congruence with this operating system we must enact 'extraction mind' or 'domination mind'. This is essentially how we advance within it. Since this system is a complex, adaptive, evolutionary system, and like all such systems wants to survive, it is self-perpetuating despite its self-termination logic. It preserves itself by drawing into positions of influence those people who best serve its purpose. As you climb, therefore, up the socio-economic ladder of capitalism, you find people who are increasingly adept functionaries of this system. Problematically this system is a death cult.

If the source code of capitalism is extraction, what context does it therefore make of the world?

Capitalism, as an operating system, turns the world, by necessity, into a mine. The capitalist gaze, intrinsic to its core logic, views the aggregation of material, energetic, metabolic, and psychic resources of the earth plane (e.g., the world) as a mine to be extracted. Extracting, within this mine, is virtuous, vis-a-viz the logic of this system. It is permissible to extract from our Mother Earth (notice that the evisceration of interiority in the English language abolishes the interiority of all beings), and we speak therefore of raw materials and natural resources rather than living stones and sovereign rivers.

It is permissible within this mining logic to extract elemental materials (e.g., metals, minerals, gases, etc.) and biotic materials. Language aligned with this project converts animate beings (i.e., trees) into inanimate objects (lumber). You will notice that linguisic alchemy whereby this system converts heinous acts, e.g., murder of animals, into palatable ones, e.g., harvesting pork. It is permissible and notionally virtuous in this system to extract labor from the bodies of the poor. That is the function and domain of corporations. It is permissible and notionally virtuous to extract ideas (intellectual property), i.e., white collar work. And it is permissible although possibly no longer considered notionally virtuous (this is why Mark Zuckerberg did not win capitalism(1)) to extract attention (e.g., surveillance capitalism & the attention economy.)

Once extracted, all of these are permitted to be enclosed, ie., productized. The gains of this process that converts common assets into enclosed forms are conferred to the owners of the respective mines that performed the extraction. These profits are cleansed, alchemically, by their magnitude, becoming virtuous by their enormity. Behold the extraction engine of the modern world.

This machine is the perfected impulse of the capitalist zietgeist: an extraction engine, psychic or otherwise. Behold the efficiency with which we can rape the earth.

⊕

I am interested in tracing, from the mists of ancestral time, and the silence before time, the birth and evolution of the denatured thoughtforms of modernity that are manifest in the death cult we are attempting to extricate ourselves from. I call it a death cult to point out what is at stake here, which is life on earth.

The mine that capitalism understands the world to be is collapsing, because we have reached the terrestrial limits of the biosphere's capacity to be extracted without modifying its foundational climatological parameters (climate crisis). In other words, we have extracted so much from this mine that it is collapsing on top of us. Our collective response to this has, so far, been to extract more rapidly.

We have, in parallel, extracted so much from our fellow humans (colonialism, racism, etc.) that our societies are collapsing. We are extracting so much from our own attention that our wellbeing is collapsing. This is the polycrisis of modernity, which, I will point out to you is the perfectly logical consequence of this operating system. This is, in fact, exactly what this operating system is designed to do. Most people do not understand this, and for many who do, we still believe it is happening over there, to someone else. It is not.

This operating system treats systemic death as perfectly acceptable collateral damage in service to its self-terminating end project. Unfortunately, only one person escapes this logic: the person who can exit the biosphere that has been destroyed. It is no accident that the richest white men on earth have become obsessed with leaving the planet.

For all the rest of us, those who do not want to live on Mars, or have the means to do so, this system is a complete disaster. No amount of material wealth on planet earth will insulate you (I'm speaking to my deca, centi-millionaire and billionaire friends here) from the consequences of this.

With this as necessary preamble to what follows, in my tracking of the originating notions of capitalism, which are now expressed with such ruthless efficiency (or absurdity) by the current system, I bring our attention to the notion of enclosure, which a foundational principle in this logic. If supremacy is its taproot, enclosure is the basement of the house we have built.

⊕

Applied to property, the enclosure (or Inclosure) of the commons was the division or consolidation of communal fields, meadows, pastures, and other arable lands in western Europe into the carefully delineated (i.e., boundaried) and individually owned and managed farm plots of modern times.

This movement began in England in the 12th Century, and proceeded rapidly in the period from 1450-1640, when its purpose was to increase the full-time pasturage available to manorial lords. During a later period, from 1750 to 1860, it was done for the sake of agricultural efficiency. Between 1604 and 1915 over 5,200 enclosure Bills were enacted by the British Parliament which related to just over a fifth of the total area of England, some 6.8 million acres.

AN

A C T

FOR

*Dividing, Allotting, and Inclosing Five Open Common Fields, commonly called* Shiffnal-Town Field, *otherwise* Pool Field, *otherwise* Drayton Field, *the* Wyke Field, *the* Church Field, *otherwise* Haughton Field, Haughton Middle Field, *otherwise* Patnal Field, *and the* Upper Field, *otherwise* Nedge Field, *in the Parish of* Idsal, *otherwise* Shiffnal, *in the County of* Salop.

I am interested here in two things primarily, neither of which have to do with property per se, but both of which are deeply connected to notions of ownership. I am interested in the notion of enclosure as it relates to the psychic (i.e., interior) landscape, and specifically our notional sense of 'possessing' a self, i.e., the implications of an enclosure paradigm on our sense of interiority as a psychic space firmly delineated, boundaried, and enclosed.

I am further interested, as I interrogate the manner in which I have been trained as an entrepreneur, in examining the way that the unconscious internalization of an enclosure model has infiltrated the assumed discourse of the internet, where colonialism is being replicated in a virtual space, and where I have been trained to create 'walled gardens', i.e., enclosure structures around our 'intellectual property' (wisdom) and then rent access to it to 'subscribers' (tenants). This latter inquiry is timely because I am in the process of inverting it, and am trying to understand how to do so.

⊕

I find the painting on the previous pages very beautiful and a little bit strange because it speaks to a yearning that I am in regular contact with these days. What I find beautiful is the ripe abundance of the harvest, and the communitarian ethos of the farmers or peasants, or villagers, whomever they are, who have come together to eat lunch as the wheat (I think it is wheat) is being harvested. Through the lens of my own deep longing, I would like to imagine that this is a depiction of a village harvesting common land. I would like to believe that this harvest does not belong to the lord of a manor who could not be bothered to come out and work in the fields, but that rather this a collective enterprise of benefit to the village.

Look at how hard they are working. The man at the left of the tree is exhausted and now fast asleep as a group of others takes their mid-day meal. I love the basket of bread, which represents the culmination of the harvest, and how everyone is sitting together on the ground in the shade of a tree that is intricately beautiful, and upon which the painter has rendered each and every leaf. This tree, strangely, occludes what I think is the church in the background, as if to say that the immediate spiritual life of the village is here, not there, locked away in some building, but right before us in the field itself with everyone seated in the shade, on the ground, together breaking bread. Here is the true communion, not indoors mediated by a professional.

I experience, in my interpretation of the painting thus, an image of the health of the village. To be honest, I'm not sure that this is really what is happening. I readily confess my yearning for a guild, for apprenticeship, for work of the hands, for community in these days of endstage capitalism.

This is Peter Bruegel the Elder's *The Harvesters*, from 1565. In an extraordinary reversal of previous representation, the peasants appear as dominant in the landscape. The curator of the Metropolitan Museum, where the painting resides, notes that if you look at the women bending over, putting together the sheaves of wheat, they have almost become them, so completely have their forms merged with the forms of the triangular sheaves. How beautiful.

Before the enclosures there is the experience, which cannot but be a psychic experience, of the commons of the village that dwarfs individual holdings. This notion of the commons fosters what Professor Darcia Narvaez calls 'the proper intuitions of relatedness.' In the commons we are part of something larger. We do not begin and end at or with ourselves, or our edges, for we are woven into a common tapestry of belonging, in which we find ourselves through sacred relatedness. Here I pause, overcome by beauty, to share this poem by Walt Whitman:

*There was a child went forth every day,*

*And the first object he looked upon and received with wonder or pity or love or dread, that object he became,*

*And that object became part of him for the day or a certain part of the day .... or for many years or stretching cycles of years.*

*The early lilacs became part of this child, And grass, and white and red morningglories, and white and red clover, and the song of the phœbe-bird,*

*And the March-born lambs, and the sow's pink-faint litter, and the mare's foal, and the cow's calf, and the noisy brood of the barnyard or by the mire of the pond-side .. and the fish suspending themselves so curiously below there ... and the beautiful curious liquid .. and the water-plants with their graceful flat heads .. all became part of him.*

*And the field-sprouts of April and May became part of him .... wintergrain sprouts, and those of the light-yellow corn, and of the esculent roots of the garden,*

*And the appletrees covered with blossoms, and the fruit afterward . ... and woodberries .. and the commonest weeds by the road;*

*And the old drunkard staggering home from the outhouse of the tavern whence he had lately risen,*

*And the schoolmistress that passed on her way to the school . . and the friendly boys that passed . . and the quarrelsome boys . . and the tidy and fresh-cheeked girls . . and the barefoot negro boy and girl,*

*And all the changes of city and country wherever he went.*

*His own parents . . he that had propelled the fatherstuff at night, and fathered him . . and she that conceived him in her womb and birthed him . . . . they gave this child more of themselves than that, They gave him afterward every day . . . . they and of them became part of him.*

*The mother at home quietly placing the dishes on the suppertable, The mother with mild words . . . . clean her cap and gown . . . . a wholesome odor falling off her person and clothes as she walks by: The father, strong, self-sufficient, manly, mean, angered, unjust, The blow, the quick loud word, the tight bargain, the crafty lure, The family usages, the language, the company, the furniture . . . . the yearning and swelling heart, Affection that will not be gain-sayed . . . . The sense of what is real . . . . the thought if after all it should prove unreal,The doubts of daytime and the doubts of nighttime . . . . the curious whether and how, Whether that which appears so is so . . . . Or is it all flashes and specks?*

*Men and women crowding fast in the streets . . if they are not flashes and specks what are they?*

*The streets themselves, and the façades of houses. . . . the goods in the windows, Vehicles . . teams . . the tiered wharves, and the huge crossing at the ferries; The village on the highland seen from afar at sunset . . . . the river between,*

*Shadows . . aureola and mist . . light falling on roofs and gables*

*of white or brown, three miles off, The schooner near by sleepily
dropping down the tide . . the little boat slacktowed astern,
The hurrying tumbling waves and quickbroken crests and slapping;
The strata of colored clouds . . . . the long bar of maroontint away
solitary by itself . . . . the spread of purity it lies motionless in,
The horizon's edge, the flying seacrow, the fragrance of saltmarsh
and shoremud;*

*These became part of that child who went forth every day, and who
now goes and will always go forth every day, And these become of
him or her that peruses them now.*

The commons is the terrain of becoming, the terrain of relating.

When we have access to the commons, when we have both the opportunity and the concomitant responsibility to tend them for the common good, our private (e.g., familial) holdings are placed within a relational web (a mycelial, dare I say, network) of relations that constrains our sense of inflated self-importance while re-inforcing our (again dare I say it) sacred and necessary obligation to operate with a view toward the best interests of the collective. We are that same child went forth…

Common lands were used for grazing, planting, hunting, fishing. These were collective resources stewarded on behalf of the community.

One of the astounding foundational errors of the European vision, arriving in the Americas, and due to the English colonizers having now been thoroughly acclimated to Enclosure because their own commons had been thieved from them, was their radical failure to understand the staggering beauty of the land they encountered as an expression of communitarian ethic of its Indigenous stewards, who wild-tended the garden/ forest / grasslands, etc., in which they resided.(2)

Indigenous people had, for millennia, been stewarding a commons, and although would not use this language, because their cosmology had evolved along different lines, its implication is similar.

In each case, the familial life was set in the context of a community, a village, one of whose many functions was to steward common resource. Within this commons grow the proper intuitions of relatedness.

⊕

I am interested in the mental, the psychic contents of this moment, in the 12th century, in Britain, when the Enclosures begin. This is at a feudal moment in Britain, and there are manorial lords, but the villagers living there have certain rights on the land, including pasture, pannage, and estovers. Pasture is the right to graze livestock, pannage the right to graze pigs in the forest, and estovers an allowance of wood that a tenant is allowed to take from the commons for the implements of husbandry, hedges, fences, and firewood. (Etymology: from the French, Estovoir, "that which is necessary."

Manorial lordships were created following the Norman conquest of 1066. Let's back up a little. The Roman Empire (hi guys, you motherfuckers again, huh?) abandons Britain at the beginning of the fifth century. Anglo-Saxon kingdoms are established in the 5th and 6th centuries: Northumbia, Mercia, East Anglia, Essex, Kent, Sussex, Wessex. These kingdoms are gradually unified during the 9th and 10th centuries, ending with the Norman conquest by William in 1066.

The origin of the manors was in the need for territorial self-defense, in particular down the east coast of the country, against successive invasions by Germanic tribes and later the Vikings. William the Conqueror created around 13,418 'manors' (areas of land administration), which the local 'Lord of the Manor' governed. The Lord of the Manor sublet this land to tenant farmers who paid the Lord rent (see our word 'landlord'.) In turn, the Lord paid taxes to the King. These manors were the pivot around which the feudal system swung.

Such a manor did not consist merely of the land. Rather, there were conveyed four distinct sets of rights. Beyond the land title, were the land rights (hunting, fishing, mining rights). Then the manorial documents. Finally the manorial title.

⊕

I want to see if I can place us here in the mindset of this moment.

I recently looked closely at an 800-year-old English manor, which was advertised for sale in *The New York Times*. 800 years takes us back, almost to this era. The manor, though immense, is dank and dark inside, the windows tiny. Roofs are strangely thatched. Stones worn into troughs through centuries of use. The sense of physical enclosure, of being totally indoors, walled off from nature, is the most powerful sense. We are deeply inside.

We are long before the birth of nation states, and the villagers are gathered close together in towns. There are no proper sewer systems. No medicine. No electric lights. The most rapid conveyance is some remnant of a cart or chariot. There is no civic infrastructure.

This movement to enclosure, a defensive movement, happens I believe for safety. To defend against the hostile.

Hostile neighbors. The ravages of winter. These are northern climes. Because materials technology at this time is not good enough to let in light but keep out cold the structures in which people lives are totally enclosed. Only the rich have windows, really. But winter will kill you, as will the barbarians from the East...

And so a trade is made, the price of which will not be apparent for many generations to come.

⊕

We say that the eyes are the windows to the soul. The mouth a doorway to the heart.

A house is always a metaphor for the psyche. One dwelling where we live is a metaphor for another dwelling where we live. What does it mean to live inside an enclosure?

What kinds of psyches develop inside of four walls, and how are they different than psyches that develop in the Living World? What is the price of being boxed in?

Ask a 3rd grader to cut through all of the political correctness, and name the archetype of European-derived modernity versus Indigeneity, and they will tell you: Europeans live indoors, Indigenous people live outside.

Do you - can you - understand what this means?

If where we live cannot but be a metaphor for the psyche, what kind of psyche develops in people who live inside?

I'll answer that: a closed psyche.

Psyche as fortress.

Psyche as defended perimeter.

This is another foundation layer, accreted beneath the known, in the basement of the psyches of the modern world.

A taproot of supremacy and a basement of enclosure.

The taproot gives rise to the schizophrenia of supremacy, the inability to have horizontal relations.

Enclosure fortifies the individual, walls us away.

It migrates out of the house into the fields, where it eats the commons, partitions the land up. It draws cleanly delineated psychic boundaries across the fields, cuts up the eco-system with the same alacrity the butcher quarters the cow.

Suddenly the child is no longer permitted to go forth. Those woods, those wilds, they belong to someone else now. They are private property. You could get shot for trespassing. And yet, not only have you lost the woods, you have lost the metaphor of the woods. You have lost the metaphor of the wilds.

You could get shot for psychic trespassing.

You must learn what belongs to you, and what does not. Stay in the house, stay in the yard. Stay in your proper place.

And so we have boxed ourselves in. Our psyches, our minds, our language, our thought forms of enclosure. Like root bound plants, we moderns: domesticated animals, primed for impending slaughter.

## 04

# Wrong Angles

# (Inverting the Logic of Enclosure, Part Two)

⊕

In 1999 Stanford University acquired Buckminster Fuller's Dymaxion Chronofile. The idiosyncratic inventor, rebel mathematician, nature architect and cosmological inquirer had treated his entire life as an experiment, and never threw away a piece of paper after his early twenties. The Chronofile, Bucky's life in paper, was measured not in pages but in linear feet of material, of which there are 1421 if I recall correctly, and which were housed in horizontal files ordered numerically in a set of rooms off the main library that were not accessible to the general public.

I had been deeply impressed by Fuller since having entered as a child the Climatron, which was an immense geodesic dome of his design at the Saint Louis Botanical Gardens that housed a rainforest: a sanctuary for me in a town I did not greatly like.

Then later again around the time when I dropped out of Yale, when I had encountered his treatise on mathematics, *Synergetics*, which I liked to walk around with and pretend I was studying,

*The Climatron at the St. Louis Botanical Gardens – Fuller's design*

but had difficulty making significant headway in.

In 2002 I volunteered to work on the Chronofile, and was accepted onto the library's volunteer staff. I was assigned to the earliest section of documents, which included, memorably, a receipt from the general store on the island in Maine where the Fuller's owned either a home, or an island, I cannot now remember, and where young Bucky had charged a significant number of items to his mother's charge account, to her displeasure. This particular receipt was scrawled with her writing, and read: *Buckminster, do not charge items to my account without my permission, for I do not like it.* Ok, I thought. He was just like any other kid.

But Fuller was not just like any other kid, and another story from his very early life makes this apparent, and perhaps lays out the groundwork for the manner in which he became an iconoclast. From a young age, Fuller had terrible eyesight. Like, really really poor. Before his vision had been tested, in kindergarten, he was given an assignment, with all of the other children, to construct a house or a bridge or some kind of structure out of toothpicks and peas. You can imagine this. The kids are sitting on the ground with trays in front of them: they have a pile of toothpicks, and a pile of green peas, and the teacher gives a demonstration and then encourages their creativity. Young Fuller couldn't see the demonstration that the teacher gave, and may not have cared about it anyway. He sits there with his toothpicks and his peas, and then makes a design decision that will shape the entire rest of his life. While his classmates, emulating their teacher, as well as the design of their classroom, the angles at which the floor meets the walls, the ceiling meets the walls, the verticality of every building they have ever seen, the axis of horizontal and vertical, the entire received visual and architectural hegemony of every structure assembled in Europe since Rome, begin to build scaffolding and structure with right angles, young Fuller, who has been studying nature, decides that he is going to build with triangles and tetrahedrons. I say decide, but does he decide, or does this just happen? Is it trial and error as he is confronted with the raw challenge, or some assertion of intellect or intuition? I do not know.

The boy sitting on the floor, in his own private world, begins to assemble a structure composed of struts and braces where each pea is the cornerstone not of an assemblage of right angles, but of sixty degree increments. His creation gets progressively more and more unusual until the entire class is gathered around him, laughing. I cannot imagine that this is pleasant, but what happens next is even more interesting, because the teacher begins to berate him, telling him he is doing it wrong. The child is five years old. And yet, strangely, he resists. Persists in his design. And then, in an occurrence that will reverberate forward through his life, he insists on keeping his strange building, and using it in the contest to see which structures can best bear weight, and he wins. Hands down. All the other houses, with their dutiful right angles crumble. Fuller's structure does not fail. It possesses superior strength.

How does this land with a child, this experience? This resistance to authority and the subsequent triumph? Many decades later, when writing in *Synergetics*, he would explain that the close packing of spheres, twelve around one, is the strongest most stable structure in Universe. This structure he names a vector

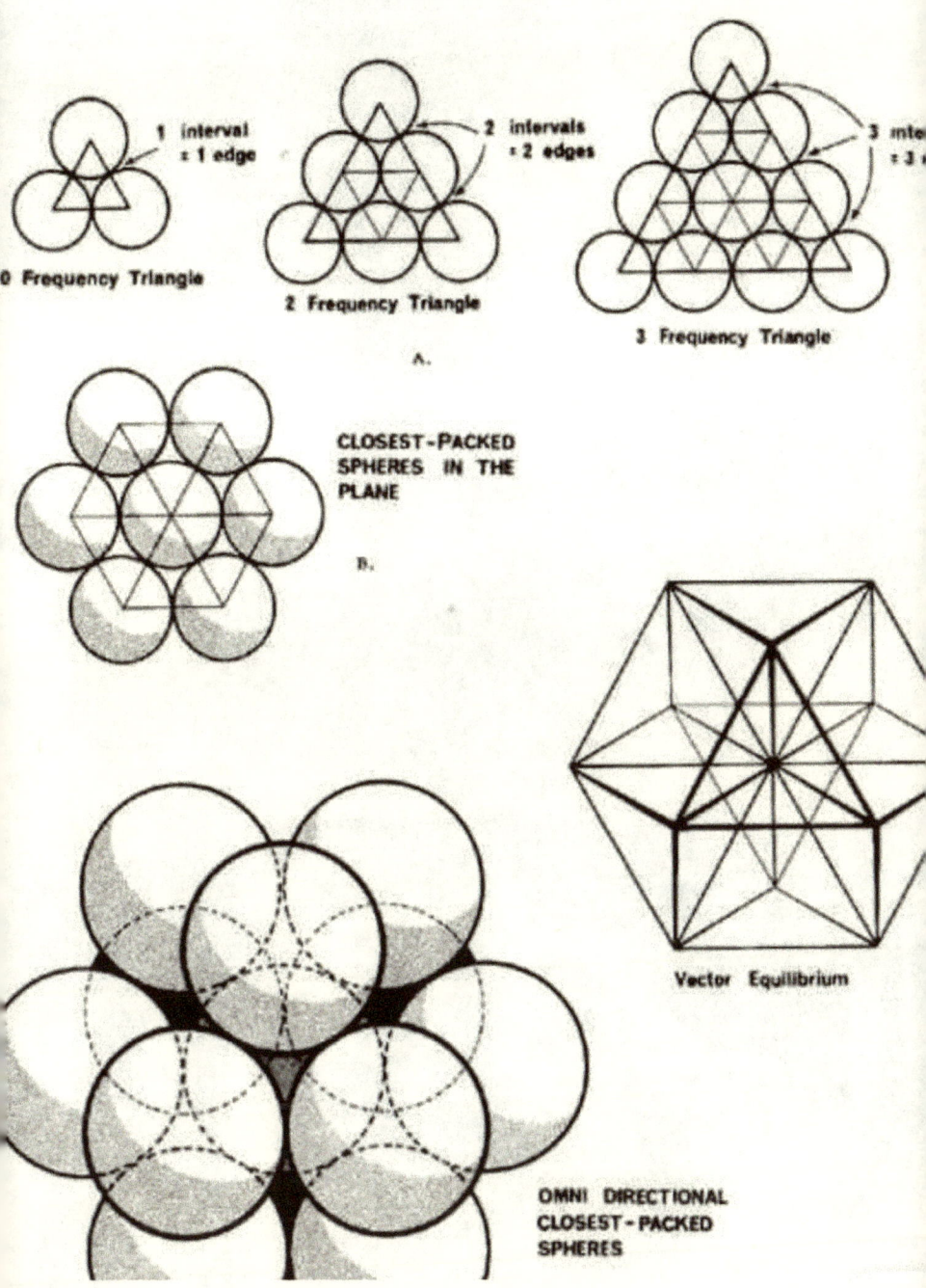

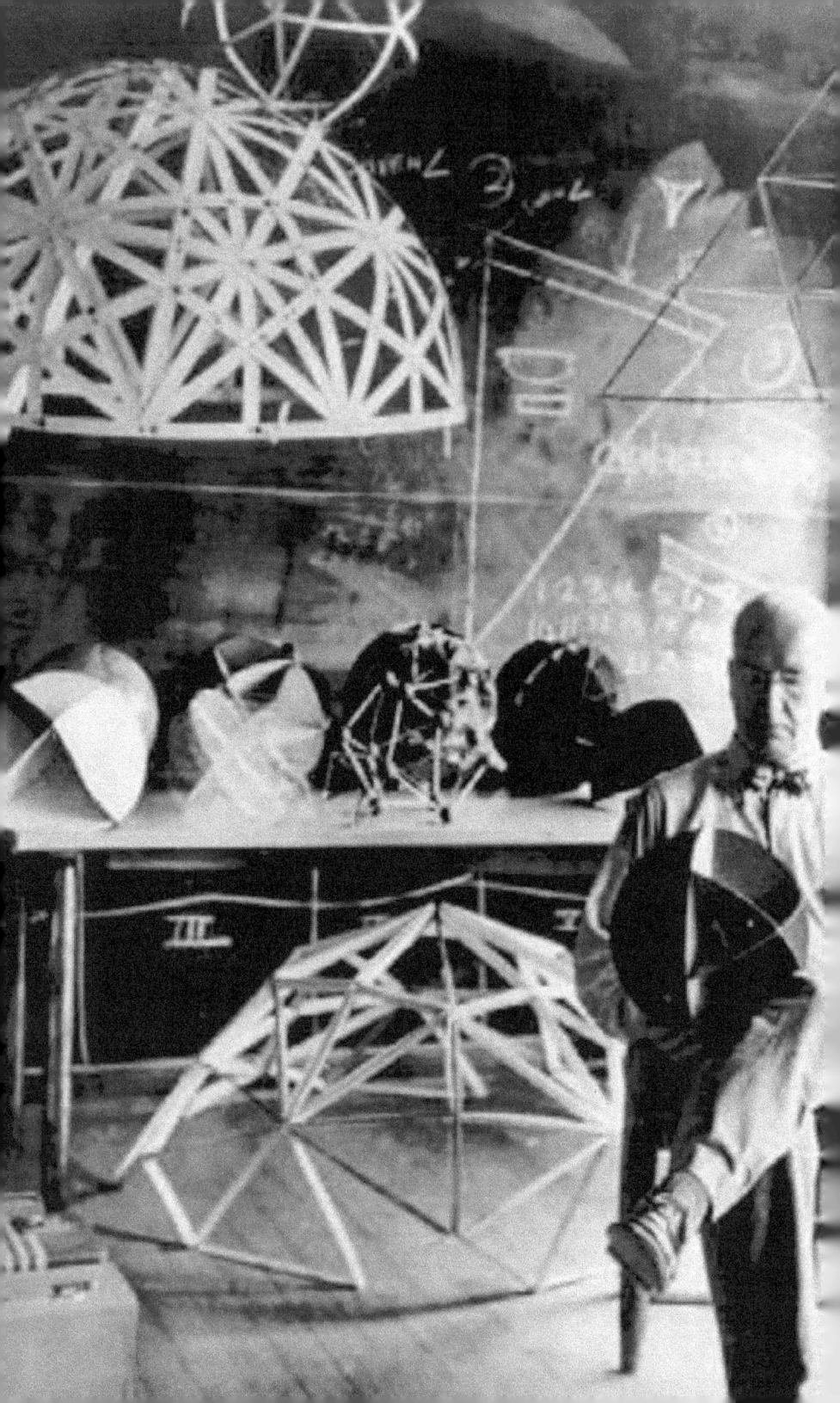

equilibrium. It is articulated through the centerpoints of twelve spheres of identical radius closest packed around a single center sphere. It is a mystical awareness, this. Twelve around one. The angles are triangles and tetrahedrons, the geometry he accidented onto as a five year old.

If Fuller's classmates and teachers had not laughed at him–if they had instead noted the brilliance of his creation and embraced it– would he have gone on to develop and articulate the vectorial energetic geometry of nature? Or did this need, this urge, this yearning arise in him particularly because of the rejection, and because he then could observe that he was right? A five year old, in an act of pure creation, steps outside the fortress of four thousand years of received mathematics. Steps back into the geometry of nature, bio-mimicked. That is what Fuller did. Synergetics are the mathematics of nature. Nature, Fuller would go on to say, would never use a strictly imaginary, awkward, and unrealistic coordinate system, by which he is speaking about our system of ninety degree axes, the horizontal and the vertical.

From *Syngergetics: The fact that 99 percent of humanity does not understand nature is the prime reason for humanity's failure to exercise its option to attain universally sustainable physical success on this planet. The prime barrier to humanity's discovery and comprehension of nature is the obscurity of the mathematical language of science.*

Stop for a moment and consider this. Have you ever seen a right angle in nature? How is it that every house, every room most people spend time in, every piece of lumber, which are the components of every house and every room, are pre-designed with right angles, when nothing in nature is made of right angles? Not a single thing. Not any part of your body, not a single tree, flower, shell, fruit, mountain, river, planet, or star. Not an atom, a molecule, a cell, or an organ. Nothing in our actual lives, nothing in our lived experience that is not made by humans is comprised of right angles, except for some kinds of crystalline structures. Doesn't this seem odd to you? Who did this? Is it possible that right angles are the wrong angles?

That the fact that we have been trained to think in them is in fact denaturing us? Mathematics, as currently prosecuted, is one of many origins of the mindbody split. One of many origins of the man-nature split. Our math is a fountain of alienation because, like a funhouse mirror, it refuses to reflect the reality of our earthly world. So how did things get to be this way? Our math is a fountain of alienation because, like a funhouse mirror, it refuses to reflect the reality of our earthly world.

Pythagoras (560-480 BCE), the Greek mathematician, was the first to prove, mathematically, the relationship between the sides of a right-angle triangle, e.g., a2 + b2 = c2. (a squared plus b squared equals c squared, where c is the hypotenuse.) But he did not discover it, as it was known to the ancient Babylonians for a thousand years before this.

| obv | | | | | | | | | I' | II' | | III' | | | I |
|---|---|---|---|---|---|---|---|---|---|---|---|---|---|---|---|
| 1 | | ta-k]i | - il- ti și - li - ip | | | | - | tim | | íb-si$_8$ | sag | íb-si$_8$ și-li-ip-tim | | | mu-b |
| 2 | | ša 1 in] | -na-as-sà-hu-ú-ma sag i-il-lu-ú | | | | | | | | | | | | |
| 3 | 1 | 59 | | 15 | | | | | | 1 | 59 | 2 | 49 | | ki |
| 4 | 1 | 56 | 56 | 58 | 14 | _56_ | 15 | | | 56 | 7 | _3_ | _12_ | _1_ | ki |
| 5 | 1 | 55 | 7 | 41 | 15 | 33 | 45 | | | 1 | 16 | 41 | 1 | 50 | 49 | ki |
| 6 | 1 | 53 | 10 | 29 | 32 | 52 | 16 | | | 3 | 31 | 49 | 5 | 9 | 1 | ki |
| 7 | 1 | 48 | 54 | 1 | 40 | | | | | 1 | 5 | | 1 | 37 | | ki |
| 8 | 1 | 47 | 6 | 41 | 40 | | | | | 5 | 19 | | 8 | 1 | | ki |
| 9 | 1 | 43 | 11 | 56 | 28 | 26 | 40 | | | 38 | 11 | | 59 | 1 | | ki |
| 10 | 1 | 41 | 33 | _59_ | 3 | 45 | | | | 13 | 19 | | 20 | 49 | | ki |
| 11 | 1 | 38 | 33 | 36 | 36 | | | | | _9_ | 1 | | 12 | 49 | | ki |
| 12 | 1 | 35 | 10 | 2 | 28 | 27 | 24 | 26 | 40 | 1 | 22 | 41 | 2 | 16 | 1 | ki |
| 13 | 1 | 33 | 45 | | | | | | | 45 | | | 1 | 15 | | ki |
| 14 | 1 | 29 | 21 | 54 | 2 | 15 | | | | 27 | 59 | | 48 | 49 | | ki |
| 15 | 1 | 27 | | 3 | 45 | | | | | _7_ | _12_ | _1_ | 4 | 49 | | ki |
| 16 | 1 | 25 | 48 | 51 | 35 | 6 | 40 | | | 29 | 31 | | 53 | 49 | | ki |
| 17 | 1 | 23 | 13 | 46 | 40 | | | | | _56_ | | | 53 | | | ki |

We know this due to a fragment of cuneiform writing on an ancient tablet, which is known as Plimpton 322, and is from the ancient city of Larsa, which was located near Tell as-Senkereh in modern day Iraq. The tablet was written between 1822-1762BCE. In 1945 the tablet was revealed to contain a complex sequence of Pythagorean triples. On the opposite page is fragment. Beneath it the mathematical transcription of the fragment. This is the fundamental relationship that Pythagoras articulated nearly 1,000 years later, demonstrating that the ancient Babylonians already possessed a complex form of trigonometry. The Babylonians, who had a sexagesimal (base 60) system of calculation, rather than a decimal (base 10), had already articulated this relationship. But why?

Dr. Daniel Mansfield, a mathematician at the University of New South Wales (UNSW) in Australia with an interest in Babylonian mathematics, explains, based on a 3,700 year old cadastral survey, which sheds light on why there was a trigonometry table in ancient Babylon.

"With this new tablet [Si.427], we can actually see for the first time why they were interested in geometry: to lay down precise land boundaries," says Mansfield. "This is from a period where land is starting to become private—people started thinking about land in terms of 'my land and your land,' wanting to establish a proper boundary to have positive neighborly relationships."

Right angles emerge because humans have entered the epoch of ownership of the earth. Right angles are a byproduct of enclosure.

So tracking back here, to the origin of right angles, takes us back to the beginning of private land ownership, which is really the origin of enclosure. Between 1900 and 1600 BCE the nature of Babylonian land ownership changes, with smaller parcels being allotted to ordinary people. Prior to this, land belonged to the palace and the temple. Now, individuals begin to own lots. There is at this time, an increase in the number of surveyors. This is a poem, from the period, in which an older surveyor admonishes a younger.

*Go to divide a plot, and you are not able to divide the plot; go to apportion a field, and you cannot even hold the tape and rod properly. The field pegs you are unable to place; you cannot figure out its shape, so that when wronged men have a quarrel you are not able to bring peace, but you allow brother to attack brother. Among the scribes, you (alone) are unfit for the clay.*

The poem refers to the tape and the rod, which modern scholars state are references to the standard Babylonian surveying tools: the unit rod and measuring rope. Yet if we dig a bit deeper, we find that these items were not merely implements of surveyors, but rather implements of royalty, and beyond that actually of divinity. These were revered symbols of fairness and justice in ancient Babylon and were often seen in the hands of goddesses and kings. Now they are in the hands of the surveyors. Let's go deeper with this. (In the image below, from a cylinder seal, note the abundance of rods and rings.)

**Illustration 3.** *Uruk Cylinder Seal, 3500–3000 B.C.E. As found in D. J. Wiseman and Werner Forman,* Cylinder Seals of Western Asia *(London: Batchworth Press, 195-), 4.*

rod is a unit of measurement, both actual and metaphorical. The rod is a standard unit of measure: the cubit rod. Anyone who has ever read, or heard the Bible read will have encountered this term– the cubit. Noah, for example, received specific dimensions about the ark he was supposed to build: 300 cubits long, 50 cubits wide, 30 cubits high. The cubit is a unit of measure in antiquity, and was derived bodily: the length from the elbow to the tip of the middle finger. Cubitum, in Latin, means 'elbow.' We can note that originally all units of measure were anthropometric. Our body, our nature itself, was the basis of the measurement.

The ancient cubit was defined as this distance from the elbow to the outstretched tip of the middle finger, and was comprised of six palms of four fingers, ergo 24 digits, i.e., base 24. We were measured against ourselves. We measured the world in relation to our own bodies. This kind of measurement system is still preserved, for example, in the measuring of the height of horses, which are measured in hands. All ancient systems of measure were referenced, we should note, anthropometrically. Yet one can imagine, easily, that there might be some variation here, as people are of different sizes. Whose cubit are we talking about?

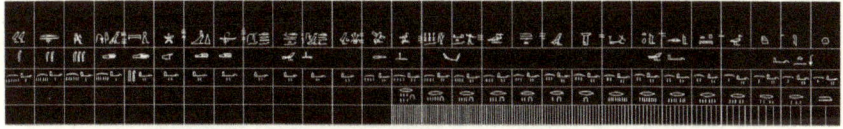

The rod, then, is a standardization of this measure. The ancient Egyptian royal cubit (*meh niswt*) depicted above is the earliest attested standard measure, and dates back to around 3000 BCE. But what do we measure? The gods who hold the rod measure the length of a human life. They are taking the measure of man. This symbol of divinity is held vertically.

In the Babylonian tradition, over several thousand years, we see these implements of divinity make their way into human hands. This happens gradually, and is depicted on stelae, cylinder seals, and tablets. In the earliest depictions, the rod and ring are held by Gods. Several thousand years later we see them in the hands of kings. This transition is marked by speculation. At first the kings revere the rod and ring, later they are holding them. I will assert here, speculatively, that by the time the surveyor poem above is written, the rod and ring had moved into the hands of the surveyor, who were performing much the same function, e.g., taking the measure of heaven and earth, and who had become, de facto, the first lawyers.

Let's dwell, for a moment, on perhaps the most famous depiction of the rod and ring, on what is now known as the Louvre stele (plundered, like the Nike of Samothrace), which depicts the Law Code of Hammurabi, in Akkadian and Cuneiform.

Here we have the Sun God Shamash seated on his throne (he wears a celestial crown that swirls about this head composed of four pairs of horns, holds a ring and staff, and has flames issuing from his shoulders) holding out the rod and ring, implements of divinity and sovereignty, toward Hammurabi. The laws? They are the rod and ring. Although Hammurabi is subservient he addresses the god directly. Even though he has his hand raised in reverence he shows that he has a personal relationship with the gods while mere mortals do not. Now take a very close look at the rod.

You will note that it is not symmetrical at both ends, but wider on the top, narrower at the bottom. It looks more, in fact, like a stake. A stake that would be pounded into the ground. The rod takes the measure of man, but it is also pounded into the ground to mark a boundary. The law code of Hammurabi, conveyed from the gods to the sovereign ruler, marks the boundaries of the kingdom, both literally and metaphorically. The law is the boundary marker. Those who marked the boundary are therefore lawyers. To survey is to prosecute the law. It is the exercise of authority over the edge of the realm.

Let us dwell, for a moment, on the ring, which may also be a rope. There are no images of a rope other than a coil of rope, which is, you guessed it, a ring. You will perhaps remember from your own study of trigonometry that no two lines can pass through the same point in a plane. This is true in the actual physical world. A circle is essentially a flat coil. The symbols of divinity, held by the gods, are a rod, held vertically, and a circle, which while depicted in images is rotated such that we can perceive it is is a circle, is actually held horizontally. Some say that the rod represents time, and the circle eternity. Some say the rod is linear time, and the circle cyclic. Some say the rod is masculine, the circle feminine. Yes to all of these.

The circle also represents horizontality. In the circle there is no above and no below. The rod is the implement of domination, of hierarchy. It is literally pounded into the ground. The circle is the implement of inclusion and relatedness. Divinity carries both implements. They are passed to sovereignty, gradually, where the sovereigns attended to the balance of the vertical and the horizontal, time and eternity. The edge (boundary marker) and the center (circle). The boundary of empire and the center of civic life.

The rod is a measurement of distance, but also of justice. The rod establishes a system of measurement. Vertically oriented, it connects the earth and the heavens. The cubit rod, unlike a staff, is too short to touch the ground if the divinity is standing, but it can touch the ground when the divinity is seated on the throne.

The rod's base rests on the ground, its tip points to the heavens. It depicts masculine authority, and is held in the right hand of sovereignty. The ring, born in the left hand, floats. Held horizontally, it conveys notions of equality, and invokes the lunar and the feminine. Imagine now, either the divinity or the sovereign aligning the two. The ring is slid over the rod, evoking the marriage of the earthly and the divine, the masculine and the feminine. An archetype of sexual congress. Viewed from the front we have a cross. A horizontal and a vertical axis. The intersections where they meet are at ninety degrees.

Yet something happens, psychically, of note, when these implements of the divine, which have become sovereign, make their way into the hands of ordinary men, the surveyors. The earth is now, on their cadastral tablets, being cut into right angle sections. Lest you imagine this being abstract, because these are farming plots, remember that an ancient Mesopotamian, standing on a ziggurat, the temples of the time, and looking out at the land, would have begun to see rectangles around them. The crops are planted to the edge of the property boundary. The Babylonians transform the world around them from a world of circles, spirals, waves: natural forms all, into a landscape of right angles. They begin to inhabit a world of rectangles. This is a concretized deviation from the ancestral baseline. This is the implementation of the imprint of the hand of man, inherited from divinity, passed through sovereignty, imprinting now on the landscape of nature. This looks natural to us because we are so accustomed to it. Yet it is very deeply strange.

Suddenly man–ordinary man– is taking the measure of things. It is one thing when this measurement, of justice, of the human span, of distance is being done by the gods, another when it is transferred to the sovereign. Yet even the sovereign is still in league with the divine. When this measurement– of justice, of time, of distance– is handed to the surveyors, something changes. We move into the bureaucratic administration of empire.

Yet lest we forget, our ancestors knew there was something magical about building. The origin of masonry is in the guilds who built Solomon's temple. Building is congress between the celestial and the earthly. It leaves the imprint of the divine here on earth. And what were these builders, holding the rod and ring, these implements of royalty, these surveyors, building? They were building temples.

And now we can turn our attention to the familiar forms of temple architecture standing in the infancy of the Eurocentric hegemony we have inherited.

Here are the Greek forms. On the next pages is the Parthenon, built in the mid-5th century BCE and dedicated to the Greek goddess Athena Parthenos ("Athena the Virgin"), generally considered to be the culmination of the Doric order.

You can imagine the sudden order of this imposed on the landscape, its verticality, the way it marries heaven and earth. Exultant. This intersection of the vertical and the horizontal planes. Imagine it against its proper backdrop: a sea of organic forms. Imagine it for a moment as the root impulse of modernity, order against a sea of chaos. Man struggling to come into power in an elemental world of overpowering forces.

This is where my architecture education began, I don't know about yours. This is the reference thoughtform.

The temple architecture, at ninety degrees, expresses this intersection, this interface between the vertical and horizontal axis, the masculine and the feminine, the earthly and the celestial, in every angle.

And yet, at the time, it would have stood out, a singular structure in rectangles against a sea of natural forms. In its time it was the anomaly. In two millenia we have inverted this relationship, flipped it upside down. We are surrounded now by rectangles. Enboxed by them on all sides.

I have always promised myself that at some point, when I had more time, I would learn Fuller's energetic vectorial geometry. Starting with triangles and tetrahedrons, rather than squares and cubes, he develops a geometry that resolves the particle-wave duality. That can explain nuclear physics with simple addition. He teaches the mathematics that nature speaks. A mathematics of triangles, tetrahedrons, fractals, spirals, waves. A mathematics of flower petals, neurocardiology, the spiral arms of galaxies.

We moderns, downstream of the wrong angle, cut adrift from anthropometric forms, a mathematics anchored in the reality of Nature, have lost our experience of relatedness through the language of mathematics, which is also the language of our 'modern' science, and like a noun-based language, no longer holds the imprint and vibration of the Living World.

We have been cut adrift from systems that foster the proper intuitions of relatedness. All around us the temple forms of an earlier era rise toward the skies, and we are lost.

05

# Toiling in a Mine

⊕

For two thousand years, since Rome, everything has been oriented toward extraction. Domination, extraction, and enclosure, these have seeped into our thoughforms, poisoned deeply the well of language, the form of desire, the shape of our yearnings. We have become blanketed in the forms of death.

It begins with alienation, expulsion from the garden, fear, a sense of scarcity. The strip mine is the allegory for the age. A rape of the surface of the living earth, the female body– an act that can only be performed with impunity once we pull the roots of the Sacred out of the earth, which happens when Rome, in feverish annihilatory glee, kills off not only the cthonic (earth-based, earth-worshipping, Indigenous) people of the region, but dismembers their gods. A bloodlust to disembowel the Sacred. It is hard to comprehend the level of death worship here, unless we understand how intoxicated they were.

There are two philosophies of war, rising arightly from what our mentor Pete Jackson identifies as their root in worldview. One set of cultures, that believes itself to exist within Nature, uses war as a means to clarify boundaries, resolve conflicts, but there are rules for war and responsibilities, as prioritization is still of Life. Blood is not spilled wantonly.

That, as you may imagine, is not the lineage we come from. We (by which I mean the modern now globalized west) come from the lineage of annihilation. The lineage that declares that if even a single member of the enemy is left alive there are seeds of rebellion, which is perhaps not untrue. You crush rebellion, in this lineage of war, through genocide. You kill them all, down to the children. If the women are beautiful enough perhaps you secret them away as concubines, but this is not discussed, as it violates the dictum. This is the lineage that believes itself to be above nature, to have 'dominion over all the creatures of the earth.'

These are our grandparents, white children, you and I. Ye who like me receive the unearned benefit of white skin privilege in this supremacy engine of a cult(ure). Remember though–white is not the color of your skin, but the mask that removes you from your indigenous self.

But how did it come to pass, this way of seeing the world? I will explain. It was the murder of the earth-based gods. The murder of the Holy Mother. It was a trick of language, the association of heaven and sky, earth and hell. It seeped into the water in vessels made of lead, through drunken debauchery, through moral corruption. Consolidation of power over, until those yielding authority were so far removed from the soil that their feet did not touch the earth, and they looked down on everything. The taproot of Supremacy is what I'm speaking about here.

Have you noticed that the Winged Victory, the Nike of Samothrace, pedestaled in the Louvre (she was stolen), and on prominent display, does not have a head. Do you think she was carved headless? No, it is not so. She was beheaded, dismembered. The Romans who culled her removed the head to deprive the God of breath, as was their habit of desecration. Does it not seem strange to you that we revere the headless goddess without mourning her murder. Has it occurred to you before I speak these words that you are witness to the murder of a divine being?

One of the mechanisms of supremacy transmission is the adoption of Nicene Christianity as the official religion of Rome. From this christianity was expunged the earthly facet of Christ's teaching: of the doctrine. Expunged were the angels of air, earth, and water: the elementals. Expunged was the great Mother herself. The prayer Our Father is inescapable. If you live in the United States you've heard it. But did you know there was another prayer? A prayer to our mother, which art the Earth? It was excised from the liturgy a long time ago.

We were taught to worship sky gods. A divinity at a remove, somewhere celestial and above. The difference between the east and the west is held in a single sentence. Ask someone from the East the question, "Heaven and..." they will answer "Earth." Heaven and earth. Ask someone from the West the same question, and whether or not they are Christian, whether or not they are a believer, they will answer "Heaven and hell." Because this is the thoughtform undergirding.

Our attention in the polarity was shifted from dichotomies of benificence: the heavenly father and the earthly mother, to a polarity of antagonism: the heavenly father and the devil. How did that happen?

The answer, I would propose to you, once again, is very simple. When your connection system is online, you experience unity. There is no need for an enemy. It is all US in here, there is no THEM. Shift across the boundary line into defense, and suddenly the physiology is polarized. We require – it is a physiological necessity – to have someone to defend ourselves against. An enemy. THE enemy.

Here is a ground zero of psychic colonization. The space designed to hold the original polarity, that of the feminine and masculine, the earth and the sky, has been corrupted, denatured. Instead of the yin-yang, instead of the balance, there resides, in its place, antagonism.

I want you to stop and dwell here, studying this original wound. Studying this psychic massacre: this origin site of your own alienation. I want you to behold it inwardly and weep. Look at what has been done to us in the name of religion.

And as you study it, I want you to understand that it is a sort of structural fulcrum. That it is a force-bearing structure in the organization of your mind, this original wound.

It is also a palimpsest, written over and over with death story. A massacre site at the origin of western consciousness. I want you to feel the echoes pulsing within and beneath it.

This story is where the West begins: it is the ejection site from relationship with All that Is. This is the story of Adam and Eve being expelled from the garden. Can you see it, how this is the same place in consciousness?

All the symbols are here. At the place where the good earth meets the sky there is a garden, and in that garden lived the original humans, speaking the original language. Until one day occurred an event.

This is the moment after which the people's thoughts no longer dwell between heaven and earth. Consider this.

It is not that evil did not exist before this. That is not what the story says. This story is the replacement of one pole- the feminine, earth-based pole of consciousness- with evil.

It is the internalization of evil.

What is the physiology of this? Defense.

This is the moment in the western psyche where we leave a baseline in connection and relatedness, and retract into defense.

With this retraction comes polarization.

Evil is internalized, and there is a *them* out there. We have moved from unity consciousness into *Us* versus *Them*.

This is a very important moment in understanding the nature of the death cult into which we have been socialized.

It is a profound differentiator of a Deathway from Lifeways.

Lifeways do not say that evil does not exist.

Jesus, himself, did not say that evil does not exist.

But the Indigenous view doesn't dwell on evil.

It is not fascinated by it. Neither was Jesus. He simply called it *unripeness*. They acknowledged and moved on.

Neither clung to lurid depictions of it, summoning it for threat and condemnation.

⊕

The story of Adam and Eve is an attempt, clothed in the language of deepest symbology, to explain an interior change in the people: an experience of alienation. Something went wrong: we don't feel right inside anymore. What could have happened? It is backcast from a received present, several thousand years ago, where people felt that something had gone wrong. People who were severely traumatized. People who had grown locked out of their bodies, turned to ice. People who were dissociated, enraged, terrified. The story is a mechanism, a form of sense-making to explain how things got to be this way. That is what stories do. This is what they are.

This particular story, in its particular contours, speaking of the first man, the first woman, a tree and a snake, is loaded with the potent elemental symbology of origins. But make no mistake: it is a death story. It tells of the death of relatedness with the Source. It is doctrinal in the death cult of modernity, a keystone bearing the weight of caternary arches, entire structures that bear the weight of configuring reality.

We have a quadrumvirate of keystones in the ceiling of this death cathedral, which is properly an ossuary. The taproot of supremacy, the transmogrification of the mother into the devil, then of darkness into evil, and the subsequent impulse to enclosure.

Look at the ceiling of the death structure thus assembled. It is

made of bones. An architecture of death upholding the modern view.

If the story of Adam and Eve is not true–and it is not true– you will need to rebuild the deep scaffolding of your awareness, because the shape of a world is architected by it, and it is the world we have inherited.

The keystones holding up the caternary arches in the ceiling of this death cathedral? It is no church at all. It is an ossuary in a mine. A mausoleum.

⊕

I invite you now to put on your archetypal antennae, your myth-making sense. I invite you to stand inwardly in a posture of meditation, of deep reflection, as though we are bent, together, over a basin of still water, water that can become a portal, a mirror, a doorway into ancestral memory, deep time.

Together let us peer downward, inward, deep, and through–let us direct our gaze, our inward gaze, the eyes of spirit, into the deep stuff of things. Let us truly see together.

What is the story trying to explain? We live in a mine, do we not? Look around you at the modern world. Despite all our apparent success, our 'elevated standard of living', all the attributes of convenience: our automobiles, endless purchasing power, access to exotic foodstuffs, can you not see the aching emptiness at the heart of things?

Can you not feel the deep suffering all around? From the wealthiest enclaves where the children are stealing their parent's pharmaceuticals to get high at parties documented on TikTok, to the meaner streets where the nitrile whiff of gunpowder cloaks itself on the back of trashstrewn wind? Can you not hear the whisper of gun violence, self-harm, murder and suicide?

Look at our mountains of trash, the islands of plastic gyring in the ocean. Walk the streets of San Francisco and listen to the homeless ranting as billionaires crack windows on the 42nd floor of penthouse apartments to breath in the desultory air of the sea and tell me we are ok. Walking through the desolate corridors of the airport in Las Vegas, the lurid neon lights of the strip in the distance tricking off windows, the penny slot machines filled with vacant-eyed travelers at two am, and you know that we are not ok. Even our best technologies: electric vehicles come to mind, require that we rape the earth, sifting through her soils for rare earth minerals or rape the ocean, plumbing her depths for polymetallic nodules. We are not ok. The children are not ok.

The story seeks to answer this question: why we toil in a mine and do not live in peace in a garden. At some time before, some time ancestral, wrapped in the mists of memory, we lived in a garden, the original garden. And we spoke a language, the original language. But now we find ourselves toiling in a mine. What is the mine?

The mine is the world after we have shifted into the fortress of defense. The fortress of defense is a contraction to avoid relationship. It is the pulling inward, a retraction. Causality is difficult to parse here, at the origin of the death cult. So many things have happened, an avalanche of consequence, and the techtonic plates have shifted. Millenia later, in the language of neurophysiology we will have a map to explain this. A map with the potency to unveil this transformation for what it is. We will be able to speak of the neuroception of danger, of lifethreat, and the way that the first creates boundary-fortification (the fortress of the ego), and the second creates boundary dissolution (the gateway to psychosis).

These sequential gates are the doorways that lead us first from the garden into purgatory, and then from purgatory into hell.

The mine is purgatory. In purgatory, we toil, the heartrate elevates, and there is the ever-present threat of danger. Of intrusion, invasion. At the perimeter of camp, darkness. Something lurking on the horizon. This is the dream landscape of danger. The blanket too short to cover our feet. This is where you wake up in the morning, fellow modern.

The purgatory of alienation is the mine we toil in.

## 06

# The Royal Garden

⊕

If you go deeply and esoterically enough into the study of sovereignty, which I recommend, you will invariably discover that the King has a garden: a royal garden. You might not think much of this initially, you might think, *Of course, a king has a castle and a garden, of course...* But if your thoughts passed over the garden like this you would be missing something important.

The garden is the kingdom. A microcosm of the kingdom. The royal garden is the place the King goes to study the Nature of reality, in Nature, with a capital N. This is what makes it a royal garden, and not just any garden.

If the King is fortunate enough, he might have a counselor or an advisor or a shaman or a magician or someone else from the cadre of the Wise who lives in the garden and takes care of it. Taking care of a royal garden is an interesting occupation, and it has less to do with planting ordered rows of crops than listening to the cosmos.

At a certain point a number of years ago, it was perhaps decades ago now, I realized that that most interesting thoughts I had–the really good ones, the really potent, deep, salient ones, almost never happened when I was thinking. Almost never. I can't remember a single really profound innovation or insight I've had when I was actually thinking. Usually, when I was gifted with an insight of depth, it came when I was not thinking. But I also wasn't generally doing busywork, or counting money, or watching Netflix, or scrolling on my iPhone. I wasn't thinking, but I was usually engaged in something I will call *dreamscaping*.

In order to dreamscape, I didn't necessarily have to be dreaming, although I have received alot of good ideas on the boundary between waking and sleep. I've had lots of meaningful experiences in the dreamtime, learned lots of things, perceived things, received warning, visited places, etc., but I don't generally derive ideas from dreams. On the threshold of dream, yes. Dreams themselves, no.

But dreamscaping, what I'm talking about, doesn't have to happen when I'm almost asleep. I've entered this stage painting, playing tennis, and in various other ways. What is usually happening is that the thing that is occupying my attention, it might involve my hands– is sort of happening in the background, with a bit of automaticity, and my attention is moving of its own volition. Not thinking, definitely not thinking. More rather on walkabout. And you know what? Do you know what place is reliably better than almost any other for eliciting this state? The wild garden.

There is something about being in a wild garden, and when I say wild garden I'm speaking not about tended rows, but someplace in pristine nature that has held onto its original form. The form doesn't matter per se. Where I live this is a forest, but it could be any eco-system. A marsh, a beach, rolling hills. It doesn't matter. What matters, I think, is getting your nervous system into congress with this original set of inputs. Why is this important?

Well–we've been here, I am told at least two hundred thousand and possibly two million years. Life is four billion years old. During this long duration of ancestry, there are a lot of inputs that have been archived deep in your nervous system, a lot of patterns. And the ones that call us home to ourselves are those that are of the Living World. I would content, therefore, that placing yourself in a wild garden puts you back into contact with the inputs of your original nature, those that foster the proper intu-

itions of relatedness. And as the proper intuitions of relatedness arrive, *voilà*, insight.

Ideas–good ones–are often pattern recognition. The archetypal catalog of pattern is deep nature. Have you noticed that you can get deeply lost staring through the leaves of a forest? Lost in the play of water over stones in a river? Lost in the tall grass if you behold it closely enough? All around us in the living world is a level of complexity–of color, pattern, texture, density, form–that is literally the context of which our bodies are made. The lacelines of your capillaries are arboreal. We are nature embodied, and in deep nature we are essentially looking into the oldest deepest mirror.

⊕

The royal garden is distinguished, perhaps, simply by this awareness: *as above, so below*. As without, so within. What makes the garden royal is not a designation *per se*, but this awareness. Black Elk, the great Oglala Lakota holy man, said the center of the Universe is everywhere, "At the center of the Universe dwells the Great Spirit. And that center is really everywhere. It is within each of us." Within this awareness, every garden is royal. The drumming of the woodpecker on that hollow tree is the heartbeat of the cosmos.

Sometimes people ask me, given my project of destorying empire, why it is that I'm interested in kingship. Isn't that where empire comes from, they ask me? But I'm not interested in kingship. I'm interested in sovereignty. And what's interesting about this to me, through an ancestral lens, is that the farther we get away from the original source cultures, the more this sovereignty gets constrained and reserved only for some elected or elite. Perhaps you could say I'm interested in the redistribution of sovereignty, only even that is approximate.

What I'm really interested in, pretty much all the time, are three things. Healing, sovereignty, and how to inherit our possible beauty. I see lots of opportunity in these three areas, because many of the modern people I know, despite their wealth, education, and opportunities, seem pretty deeply beholden to disease, pretty deeply ensnared by systems actively removing their liberation, and pretty far from their possible beauty.

This beauty is, I believe, connected to purpose and authencity, and is not, generally speaking, trending on TikTok. Its a highly individual affair. This is probably because, algorithms be damned, no two humans are exactly alike. If we don't know ourselves we can be convinced that we are, we can be aggregated into narrow demographic slices and spoonfed things that align with our expressed preferences, but this isn't beauty. The kind of beauty I'm talking about is raw, and elemental, and powerful and sometimes frightening. A lot of people will be put off by your actual beauty because it inconveniences them. It inconveniences them because it tends to reflect the ways in which they have not inherited their own possible beauty, and this makes alot of people uncomfortable. Beauty like this is not commodifiable.

The reason a King, and I'm using this term for simplicity, but I could use the term Queen, or simply sovereign, because what I'm talking about has nothing to do with gender, has a royal garden, is because the garden won't lie to them. Actual historical sovereigns were having all kinds of sunshine blown up their asses, but Nature, with a capital N, doesn't care about that, and won't lie to you. A tree won't tell you something to make you feel better about yourself. Nature calls it as it is.

Operating from sovereignty, we encounter all sorts of conundrums, all sorts of situations where the playbook of the received order of things doesn't seem to constitute an adequate or appropriate answer, and so after consulting with various advisors from the cadre of the Wise, the sovereign might take some time in the royal garden to ask the question of Nature. If the sovereign is thinking about it, usually the answer will not come, but if the sovereign places themselves in the context of the Reality of Nature, capital R, capital N, with the disposition to listen, to receive insight, sometimes they are blessed thusly.

What is usefully confounding about this notion, to our modern sense of self, is the awareness that thinking, cogitation, the activity of the brain, the mind, which tends to structure itself through words, images, etc., happens inside the mind. And you will notice that what I'm talking about here is not happening inside anything. It is happening *between*. In a relational field.

What the sovereign needs to know is not inside the sovereign's head. If it were, the sovereign would already know it. It is not entirely outside of it either, but in the relationship between the sovereign's consciousness, and the proper context to foster intuitions of relatedness.

There is that phrase again: the proper context to foster intuitions of relatedness. A context that fosters the proper intuitions of relatedness is a context that allows us to FEEL the necessary interdependencies of the Living World. Let's start out by listing a number of contexts that do not foster the proper intuitions of relatedness. How about living indoors? Living in buildings composed of rooms of right angles? Living in a rectilinear grid of streets? Buying our food at the grocery store encased in plastic. Filling up at the gas station. Sitting in rush hour traffic. Doomscrolling Facebook. Watching television. Playing online poker. Tweeting. Virtual reality. The metaverse. Cryptocurrency. Playing the stock market. Getting takeout. Texting. Politics. I could go on... What does foster proper intuitions?

Multi-age community. Village. Being outside, especially in places where original landscape is intact. Being in the water. Walking barefoot. Making things with your hands. Engaging in conversation. Doing nothing. Taking naps. Rest. Watching people's faces when they talk. Doing things in real life. Creativity. Gifting. Proper intuitions are fostered largely by analog activities.

Activities and contexts that foster the proper intuitions of relatedness are relational. There is congress, through them, across the boundary that separates our interiority from the world. We don't fall back into isolated self. We connect across the boundary. In order to do this, we have to be experiencing enough safety to be open to experience. Many modern people are not. This is part of where sovereignty is related to healing. If we are defended against the world we don't relate.

⊕

Let's talk for a moment about the sovereign's responsibilities. The sovereign is responsible for a kingdom. This is, archetypically, something much larger than they are, something complex, something that they cannot control. There is some linguistic nuance that emerges here, and it is important to our project, because there are various words for sovereign that have been translated as chief, or king, or later Emperor, but they mean very different things. The Greek word for emperor, *Archon*, shares the same root as architecture, and denotes authority derived from structure. In this case, the Emperor is an agent of control. But what we are concerned with here, the lineage of sovereignty I'm discussing, has a different etymology and a different cosmology.

This kind of sovereignty is not so concerned with power over, but power *with*. This is the kind of sovereignty that Lao Tzu describes in the Tao te Ching. The kind where, when the activity has been accomplished, the people feel that they have done it themselves. This is a kind of sovereignty expressed through creating the proper context of relatedness that brings out the sovereignty in the people. Where sovereignty goes viral. And when sovereignty goes viral its close companion is genius, which, in truth, and etymologically, comes from Nature.

Thus the sovereign, as one tasked with the responsibility for creating the context in the realm that brings it to its greatest collective potential, goes to the royal garden to educate themselves about reality.

I want to bring your attention to something more broadly thematic, which is an undergirding framework of this text. What I am proposing to you is that modernity is a mine. The entire apparatus of the modern world is set up as an extraction engine. What I'm trying to do is help us transition out of this labyrinth of death, make our way out of the subterranean depths of modern culture, which is where we are stuck precisely because we've disavowed the cthonic, the earth-based, and the destruction wing of creation (to flee depth, the underworld, and death is to run headlong toward it). The path out of the mine is toward the garden. The garden is the metaphor and the model we want and need. Do you remember the original garden? We are told that we got kicked out of it for bad behavior, but that's not what actually happened. By the time we wrote that story, we were already alienated.

What I'm describing for you here is the metaphor of the garden as context, and part of where I'm going to take this is a meditation on work, because as you can imagine, the sovereign is busy. They have a kingdom to run. And yet, strangely–it's not exactly strange–they are spending alot of time out here in the royal garden. Why is that?

⊕

The most expert gardener I know, who is technically a master gardener, the one time I called him that became visibly and squeamishly uncomfortable. He said, *No, actually I'm a servant gardener.* Although at the time I thought he was being simply self-effacing, what he was saying is deeper than that. The royal gardener doesn't go around doing stuff. He doesn't, whimsically, decide to change the landscape. If you watch him walking around in the garden, you might notice him using a clippers to cut a single blade of grass. Watch this for awhile and you are tempted to think it is inefficient: like picking up single grains of rice with chopsticks. But let your gaze trail a few steps behind him and you start to see a level of beauty emerging that rivets the eye. It was beauty that was already there, more or less. But a single blade of grass removed here, the branch of a shrub pushed back there, and suddenly something else is coming forward, something more vivid, something deeper rooted, something more beautiful, even.

The strange thing about watching the royal gardener work is that after she is finished you cannot tell that she did anything. You cannot see her interventions. A branch is gone here. A stalk there, a blade of grass missing. But you cannot see them. She has taken away what was obscuring the highest expression in the garden. She is like a stone sculptor more than a painter. She removes what gets in the way. And she does this rather slowly, if you ask me. Watch her work, and sometimes you cannot tell that she is moving. Ask her what she is doing and she will look at you quizzically and explain that she is studying the garden. She is asking with her eyes. Asking permission, asking questions, listening, feeling, looking for patterns. She is not *doing* anything. The doing happens through her.

How is it that the work that most of do in the modern world has become divorced from what is most meaningful to us? How is it that we've traded our sovereignty, and our possible beauty for security? For the steady paycheck? It sounds like I'm condemning, but I'm not. I know how. It's because we live in a mine. A debt prison. It's because after paying for college, and graduate school, and housing, and with the cost of living in this (any) damn city- everything so fucking expensive these days...It's because some of us send money home to our parents, pay tuition for our children's schools, don't have health insurance, pay the doctor's bills out of pocket. It's because our kids need braces, and a math tutor. All of this stuff we need help with because there is no village, and there is no safety net, and everything has become transactional. And if you don't pay your credit card bill on time that shit goes to a collection agency. The institutions are quite serious about getting paid, are they not?

And so this inkling in the direction of possible beauty, the dreaminess, the way that you felt playing with watercolors for the first time, the stunning wash of color and the vitality you felt–that gets brushed aside because who makes a living as a watercolorist? Do you know anyone who pays a mortgage painting watercolors? It's about like that.

And yet, at what cost? Here we are in the royal garden, where the royal gardener has time, and what is she doing? Almost nothing. Her movements are pregnant with *almost* nothing. And yet the whole kingdom is waiting in them. Because she is creating the context in which the sovereign will come, and sit, and stare, and let their eyes relax and ask a question out into the pure emptiness of the womb at the center of the Universe, and because the center of the Universe is everywhere, including this garden, the insight will come.

And there are a few people, still, who have managed to set their lives up, through luck, or contrivance, or some good fortune, so that they can have moments like the royal gardener, who is not rich, but also is not afraid, and has sovereignty over her time.

Nearly everything that I can think of that is beautiful– and I mean beautiful, beautiful–pierce your heart beautiful, shake you to the core, beautiful– requires sovereignty in time. No one makes a masterpiece in a rush. Even a torrent of creativity comes with its own innate cadence. Because genius comes from Nature, and nature only comes to us when we are *relating*. And relating is not stressed. It is not distressed.

And so how do we carve out, with the demands of the mine all around us, the crushing pressure of it, the weight of debt–how do we carve out a sacred space in which to create, a sacred space in which to experience enough safety to reclaim our sovereignty?

Because the truth of the matter is that we've been fooled. Lied to. Distracted and distanced from ourselves. I've been taught, for example, to throw away all of the scraps of leftover food. I've been taught this from a young age. And then you go to the grocery store and heirloom tomatoes are $7.99 a pound. And yet–if I step out of the mine for just a moment, reclaim sovereignty of time, cultivate the proper intuitions of relatedness I realize– *wait a minute*. If I take those scraps of leftover food...The trimmings from the vegetables we didn't use...the tops of carrots, the extra leaves from the cauliflower. The coffee grounds. That hunk of moldy cheese. The stale bread. If I take all of that and I mix it with a little bit of earth, a little bit of water, and I put it outside, it will turn into soil. A miracle right under my nose. If I take the eggshells I have been trained to throw away, and I break them down (this I learned from a Hawaiian Indigenous farmer), and I heat them a little bit to dry them out, and I put them into a jar with rice wine vinegar, a chemical reaction will take place, and the vinegar will pull the free calcium out of the shells. And if I then take the soil I have made, and I plant seeds, and I water them with this homemade fertilizer...then I won't have to spend $7.99 a pound on heirloom tomatoes. My tomatoes will be beautiful.

Life is waiting, all around us, to remind us of who she is. Nothing in life is linear. It doesn't move in straight lines, organize in right angles, or scale. The only things that scale in nature are viruses and cancer. Goodness doesn't scale. A garden doesn't scale. A garden grows.

And look around. The sun is pouring down benediction and light, free for the harvest if you have the right kind of collector. A solar panel is a pretty good solar collector, but a plant is the *perfect* solar collector. Right here, underneath our noses, waiting to be noticed by someone who has enough sovereignty over their time

to see through the distraction.

What I'm trying to take off, to step out of, to free myself from, to free us from isn't only the debt–although assuredly I am trying to take that off. What I'm trying to take off is the mind. The mind of modernity that has been programmed to see the world as a mine. That has been programmed to make bets in that direction. That gets seduced, again and again by something just out of reach, the next big thing, when what is right here in this moment, touchable with these two hands, feelable and knowable with this heart and this body, is right in front of me.

This the royal gardener has discovered, and the King as well. There is the pomp and circumstance of the realm, coronations, visits from ambassadors, meetings of the war cabinet, the diplomacy and all of that. But the sovereign sitting on the throne–and the thone is not an object, not a chair, but the sovereign's seat–which is in the body, is in fact in the royal garden.

Reality is a garden, not a mine. And what you and I and all of us need to figure out, right now, is how our thoughts, relatedness, and behavior would change if we understood that.

## 07

# Death's Head

⊕

On a day in May a moon ago I woke after having worked thirty-one days in a row, and, taking a shower, realized the last time I had worked at this intensity for so many days was during a war. The moment I thought this there appeared so vividly in my mind's eye the image of a battle, replete with sounds and smells, shouting and metal scraping and guttural screams and the salt smell of the sea, the colors of it, many troops in crimson, the close proximity of people fighting hand-to-hand, that I was, for the better part of a minute, there.

Later in the day, driving to our nature preserve, I ran over a rattlesnake. I did not do this on purpose. It was stretched out in the road, and I was going too fast to stop. I got out of the car, a hawk called, and when I got close to the creature I saw from the arrowhead shape of its skull that the snake was venomous. Then I saw the rattle. I returned to my car, took an axe from the trunk and cut the snake in two. I picked up the head, and was astonished by how soft, how supple the skin was. It was deeply beautiful. I had never held a rattlesnake before. They are not something you pick up.

Other snakes I have held in my life, but they were scalier, none with a velvet skin like this. In its diamond-patterned beauty, fawns and browns, and its softness it was lovely to hold. Be-witching. Deeply strange. How could something so dangerous be so soft? I wanted to study the head as well, and I wanted to look into the snake's eyes, which were wide open, to see what might be writ there, of what mysteries it might tell. I took the head and I put it in the back of my car, on the seat, and I finished the drive.

About ten minutes later, after unloading the lumber I had brought to the land, I went back to retrieve the head. I was looking at it, the pale yellow-whitish underbelly lying on the seat, the elaborate tilework of the underside of the jaw, when it flipped over and revived. This was so eerie it took my breath away. The snake had a gaping tubular hole at the end where the body had been: I could see straight into the body cavity, which oddly, in retrospect, was not bleeding. There had been, in fact, almost no blood at any time. The snake's eye had been, and remained, wide open. Thus the reptilian gaze. I took a broom from the trunk of my car and knocked the snake out onto the grass. Then I got the axe and killed it a second time. This time I cut the head off just behind the skull. Again, no blood.

Unnerved and jangly, I took the axe, and hiked, bare-chested, the quarter-mile back to where I had killed the snake the first time. I knelt in the dirt road, and cleaved off the rattle in a stroke. This I picked up, and brought back to the car, where I set both the head and the rattle on a wooden board. I wasn't going to touch the head again until I was damn sure it was dead dead. I found myself pacing around for some time, restless. I was suddenly the possessor of the head of a rattle snake, and its rattle, and though I had some sense of their talismanic import, and also some sense of their relatedness to being at war, and my reverie in the shower, I confess that I wasn't sure what to do with them.

I went and sat on the land and breathed into my feet and through the earth until I could feel myself on the inside without shaking and became still enough that my thoughts stopped. And then, for some reason, it became obvious to me that I needed to place the objects in a sacred box.

A couple of hours later, when I was convinced the snake was actually dead I picked up the head. Using my finger and thumb I squeezed it from behind, laterally, and when I did so the jaws opened and the fangs, as though they were spring loaded, rotated out into striking position. It had a premonitory quality, this hinge-like motion. It accorded with the visual I have either seen

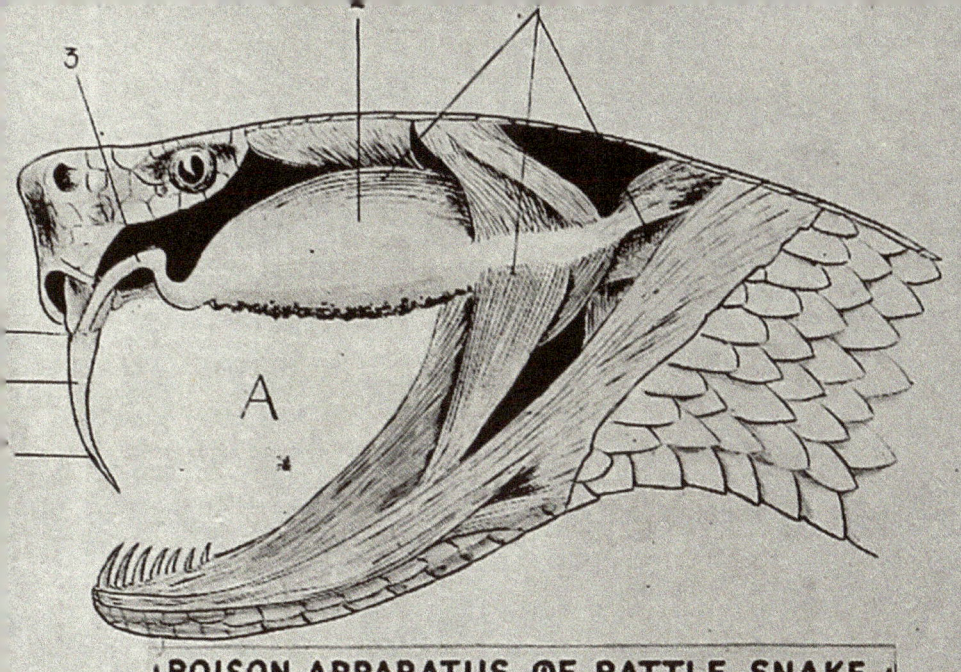

**·POISON APPARATUS OF RATTLE SNAKE.·**

The fangs, when the mouth is closed, rest folded up against the roof of the creature's mouth. If they did not it would stab itself every time it closed its jaw. As I held the jaw up in the forest sunlight, studying death at such close proximity I saw something astonishing. Behind each fang was another structure. It twinned the fang, with the same arc, but this needle was no wider than a human hair.

The fang is the bite, and the fangs are hollow on the front side, which is the mechanism by which the venom is conveyed. But what was this other structure, a structure only visible in certain light, fine as a hair? A structure no one had ever told me existed. Was this the true conduit of the deadly? I have scoured the literature now, a library of images, and there are no pictures I can find of this second set of structures. They do not exist. Yet there they were, a pair of them, just behind the fangs, clear and obvious on very close inspection, vivid as life.

And so I ask you, how is this like the modern world? What is the death's head that must be killed twice? And if modernity, in its necrophiliac incarnation in the death cult of capitalism, this empire inherited from Rome, this great destroyer of life, wounds with the fangs, what is the role of the nearly invisible hairlike needle behind it?

The head, after several days in the box began to stink, and so I boiled it and scraped all of the flesh off. It sits now in a sacred box on my computer, begging the question, each time I sit down to write– can you not get seduced by the modern world? Can you remember that at its center is a death's head? How many times will you have to kill it before it is dead?

## 08

# At the Origin of Consciousness: A Crime Scene

⊕

I didn't get to meet Terrence McKenna while he was alive. I was, however, a grateful recipient of his writing, placing me squarely in the path of influence of his immense linguistic facility and playfulness, which was deployed in service to a vision of consciousness that was as deeply strange as it was plant-inflected. In the lineage of the great ethno-botanist Richard Evans Schultes, and like Shultes' student Wade Davis, McKenna made his way to the Amazon, in addition to other places around the world, to apprentice himself to plants. In 1992, in a book called *Food of the Gods*, he promulgated a theory, which became known as the Stoned Ape theory, that the deep origin of the human species, the transition from Homo Erectus to Sapiens, and the concomitant revolution in consciousness that he proposed was of a cognitive nature, occurred as a result of earlier humans ingesting *Psilocybe cubensis*, a type of psilocybin-containing mushroom that likes to grow in cow dung. McKenna proposed that sometime around 100,000 years ago, when our Homo Erectus ancestors were following herds across the savannah, we began eating psychedelic mushrooms that grew in the dung in their wake. This, he proposes, is the origin of human consciousness.

Basically, we became cognitive giants by plucking psychedelic morsels out of piles of bullshit.

I didn't know McKenna personally, but I have friends who did. The stories I have been told about him, including a number of stories that he, as well as his brother Dennis wrote about, make numerous mentions of him taking what is probably an unfortunate choice of words to describe this activity, but is nonetheless known as taking heroic doses of hallucinogens. A heroic dose, which I would propose to you that without proper guidance is more likely to be a foolish, dose of psychedelics, is one large enough, generally speaking, to dissolve the containment structure that has become known to most of us through therapy-speak as ego.

McKenna, by his own admission, had a propensity to take extraordinarily large doses of psychedelics without guidance. He was a self-described psychonaut, fearless to his own detriment. One of the problems, for someone who is deeply cerebral, in taking immense doses of hallucinogens outside of the context of a wisdom lineage, and without proper guidance, is that it is somewhat like getting into a rocket ship that you cannot steer, and blasting off, and we have a hard time not attributing significance to what passes by the window of such a cosmological transit. Yet you could end up literally anywhere in the universe on such a trip.

The structure of consciousness can be so altered, in these experiences– what we sense, feel, see, and interpret as a result of them so deeply otherwordly and potent- that it is not difficult to believe what we have experienced is real.

In 1980, in a book published by the anthropologist Michael Harner called *The Way of the Shaman,* the author speaks about a series of experiences he had drinking ayahuasca where he gradually became aware of more and more visions and information being presented to him by "giant reptilian creatures reposing sluggishly at the lowermost depths of the back of [his] brain". "I could only vaguely see them in what seemed to be gloomy, dark depths," he explained. He was given information reserved for the dying and the dead, he was told.

The "reptiles" projected a visual scene in front of Harner, which showed the creation of life on earth. But first before that life there were hundreds of "large, shiny, black creatures with stubby pterodactyl-like wings and huge whale-like bodies" that dropped from the sky and landed on the barren landscape. Their heads were not visible (shades of Voronezh and even Lake George in Australia). These beings were fleeing from enemies from outer space. They created life on earth "in order to hide within the multitudinous forms and thus disquise their presence."

Harner learned that "the dragon-like creatures were thus inside of all forms of life including man (almost like DNA, although at the time, 1961, Harner knew nothing of DNA). They were the true masters of humanity and the entire planet", the "dragon-like creatures" told Harner. He was caught up in a struggle between the aerial ship with the "bird" people taking his "soul" and the "dragon-like denizens of the depths." As he felt he was about to die Harner was able to cry out "medicine", whereupon in the real world the Indians frantically sent about making an antidote. A powerful being appeared before Harner to protect him from "the alien reptilian creatures".

Simultaneously the antidote to "the little death" drink [ayahuasca] was given, and the dragons and "the soul boat" disappeared. While the antidote eased his condition, Harner continued having "many additional visions of a more superficial nature... I made fabulous journeys at will through distant regions, even out into the galaxy; created incredible architecture; and employed sardonically grinning demons to realize my fantasies." He finally slept until waking surprisingly refreshed and peaceful the following morning.

Harner found that he could remember all of the experience except for "the communication from the dragon-like creatures". Eventually he was able to rember it. He was then seized by a fear that he should not know this material, that it seemed intended only for the dying. His remedy - he quickly told others, including local missionairies - who were startled by the similarities with parts of the Book of Revelations. This came as a surprise to Harner - an atheist.

Harner also sought advice on his "vision" from "the most supernaturally knowledgeable of the indians, a blind shaman who had made many excursions into the spirit world with the aid of the "ayahuasca" drink. The shaman said of Harner's "masters of the earth", "Oh, they're always saying that. But they are only the Masters of Outer Darkness."

The most vivid experience of Harner's life, it turns out, was a hallucination. You can't believe everything you think, or everything you are told. *I am the lizard king, I can do any thing.* No, in fact you are not. That is bullshit.

⊕

It is of critical importance to be very discerning in which thoughts we listen to. Not all of them, perhaps not that many of them, are true. Thinking, the way most of us do it, provides very tenuous access to truth. McKenna was an extremely cerebral person. He identified with thinking. Thinking as being... He wouldn't take issue with Descartes' maxim, which I flatly reject. He encounters the plants, and they gift him an amplification of his own propensity for extraordinary hypothetical musings, which was quite keen to begin with. These they color with synesthetic vividness and character with insight. Is there some kernel of truth to them? Perhaps, I do not know. Is it possible that this happened? Certainly.

Was our eating of mushrooms out of dung *THE* catalytic event in the origin of a 'modern' consciousness? Was he encountering the origin of the species, or simply seeing himself? Each of us, the humans who I've spoken to, in an original encounter with the entheogens, has some version of this moment.

I had a moment like this the first time I smoked marijuana, which isn't even an order of magnitude approaching the crisis that can be induced by a psychedelic. In some moment, you suddenly become conscious of your own mind as a structure, and you find yourself beholding it from some vantage that is not the same as how you ordinarily live within it. Is this the origin of consciousness?

There is a disruption of the ordinary stream of self, and the dimension of awareness changes. We realize that we are not perceiving reality, we are filtering it through an engine that is mind. We cannot realize this until we step out of our ordinary mind. Is this the dawning of consciousness in the species? Or in McKenna? Is it ancestral memory or waking dream? Is it the mushroom that is important? Or is it the crisis it induces that is important?

Terrence McKenna died of brain cancer. My impression is that the brain, which likes to make thoughts and imagery, is not the most useful organ in which to center oneself when interacting with these forces: that the indole alkaloids, which are the chemical carriers in the plants that unlock such realms, are more usefully metabolized with our center of gravity in the heart. And yet that pushes against the western inclination to center the world in the seen (even be it inner seeing) rather than the felt.

Another theory of the origin of consciousness, one less hallucinogenic, yet no less brain-centric or vision-contingent, in its way, comes with Julian Jaynes, whose 1977 book *The Origin of Consciousness in the Breakdown of the Bicameral Mind*, suggests that the ability to introspect, which Jaynes' asserts as the origin of the uniquely human consciousness, is a byproduct of language and culture. He suggests that it arises specifically from metaphor, including metaphors of vision inwardly applied. Jaynes is concerned with introspective real estate: the origin of mind-space.

In both theories there is some catalyzing event that sparks the opening of a new inward horizon. There is a break in some plane of consciousness: the sudden arising of a new dimension, a relationship to a novel interior. We – our awareness – is conveyed, is birthed, discovers itself in a new space. We wonder: How did that happen?

And yet both of these theories are concerned with mental space. I find it interesting to notice that both of these theories, implicitly, build on the notion that consciousness is cognitive in nature. That its principal attribute has something to do with thinking, or the space in which thinking unfolds. I also find both theories impose a modern worldview invisible to the theorist onto a geography of ancestral consciousness that was in all likelihood unlike what either man was capable of imagining.

I find it unlikely that speciation was driven solely, or even primarily, by proto-hominids tripping balls, even if some of them undoubtedly did that. I find it unlikely that introspection is the advent of interiority.

I find myself wondering, personally, if the origin of consciousness, as it were, is not with introspection, but with *interoception*. Not with mind-space, but with felt-space. And yet, I will also propose to you, that in my own experience the origin of consciousness is a crime scene. I mean this archetypally, as it relates to the origin of consciousness in the species, as well as personally, which is an arena I feel more qualified to comment upon. But, for shits and giggles, let's start with the wide, the vast, the speculative, and then we'll come closer in.

As I've told you before, I am a tracker. I have friends who track animals, and I have friends who track history. I track connection, and part of what I'm up to here in these essays is tracking back into the mists of deep time to notice the source frequencies of kinship, and how we deviated from them, for we've erected edifices of nationhood, law, economy, and knowledge that are categorically deviated from Life. How we've come to be living in a death cult, which is what any sober analysis of our modern living program will tell you it is. I won't pretend to have certainty about any of this. I'm tracking background radiation emanating from behind the origin stories of our culture. What I'm listening with is not cognition at all.

I've spent a fair amount of time feeling into, and reflecting on the event described in the Bible as the Fall. This is not because I'm overtly interested in the Bible. It is because I lived the experi-

ence of falling out of harmony with All That Is at seven years old, and I recognized my own life in that story. I could have written that–I just wouldn't have blamed it on a snake and a woman.

My particular story is that I grew up in an essentially non-indigenous small band, in a spiritual community my parents were part of, in a tiny rural town in the Connecticut River valley. My earliest consistent memories are of this place, and although it is perhaps a bit rose-colored in my personal rearview mirror, my experience of living there was some version of living in paradise. I loved that community, and that place, in such a deep, original, wild-hearted, reverent and unguarded manner that it was not in the realm of possibility to me that it could be taken away from me, until some time after the moment when it was.

In 1982, when I was seven years old, the US economy entered a recession, my father lost his job, we packed our lives into boxes, and I got into a Ryder truck with him and drove out of the garden of Eden and into my life. I didn't know this is what happened until much much later. My experience of the event, for most of my adult life, was that when I was seven years old I drowned. Some part of me–perhaps the best part of me–simply died. I didn't drown in water. My suffocation was being removed from my original context, uprooted, potted in emotional and cultural soil that couldn't nourish me, and being unable to grieve. That was what took away my oxygen. I was stunned by loss, a grief so immense that it froze me to the quick.

I didn't have language for any of this exile at the time. I was seven years old. I did not know how to express this, and no one in my family noticed. Part of me was dead, and not anyone in my world had the wherewithal to reflect this back to me. No one said, "Good morning Gabriel. I can't help but notice that today you seem to be hauling around some percentage of a corpse, whereas yesterday you were alive." That would have been useful to me, I think. To have had someone notice this. Instead, it took me thirty-five years to figure out what happened, and to resuscitate the part of myself that was dead, which turned out not to be dead, only there is some mystery in this, because it was until it wasn't.

Returning for a moment to this notion of interoception as both the origin of consciousness, and the byproduct of a crime...

When we are in harmony with All That Is, there is no interoception, because there is no boundary separating what is inside from what is outside. There is just awareness. It is a non-dual state. Interoception is, therefore, a hallmark of the falling out of kinship. The origin of consciousness, in the sense that modernity is using it, is actually the origin of alienation. It is the origin of the untethered bounded self. I'm going to take you through this very slowly, because it is so important.

I have explained in the book *The Neurobiology of Connection*, what we (Hearth Science) understand, through our research, about the second neuroceptive gate, which is the gate at the threshold of the shutdown state. We refer to this gate as a gate of boundary-dissolution. Usually we crash into this gate under the full influence of rage or terror, and this impact vaults us out of the center of self as the boundary dissolves. It is, in other words, a terrifying dissociative experience. Yet there are experiences in meditation, reported with frequency across many different spiritual lineages, of boundary dissolution without displacement. In less formal contexts, the most everyday of these experiences, for many people, happens during sex. We are immobilized, yet without fear. It is called 'making love' because if this happens in a heart-centered way, through this boundary dissolution, we can unite with another. If this Other is All That Is, the universe entire, we are in the realm of spiritual experience. Union.

When we are in that Union, we can't use the word interoception, in its ordinary sense, because if we are connected with Source, there is not a boundary inside of which our feeling is constrained. We simply feel. This feeling harmonizes with the universal breath. The universe herself hums; she inhales, exhales. She expands and contracts.

In our day-to-day lives, most of us it would seem, cannot reside in such a state, and therefore exist within the sensing confines of a body, if we are not shut down interoceptively in such a way that we cannot feel ourselves from inside.

This ability to feel ourselves from inside, this inward listening, as it were, this utilization of our body as a felt interior, as an apparatus of perception, an embodied field of awareness...interoception, in other words...this, I would propose to you IS consciousness. Not introspection, but interoception. This bottom-up, embodied, generally though not always co-terminous with the body, present-moment-centered feeling of electric vitality humming through a dimensional space. This is consciousness. Ego not required.

If this is our operating system, then ego, in the modern sense of identity–is not needed. My favorite definition of ego: a contraction to avoid relationship. (from Franklin Albert Jones, via Arthur Baker.) Ego is, dare I say it, the habit of contracting to shut out a hostile world.

Ego is the boundary tightening we engage NOT to be in kinship. A boundary fortification reified through neurological habit and storied through narrative into identity.

If the operating system we are running is interoceptive–the feeling of what is–and look: here is a magnificent vagal neural architecture placed to support this, seventy percent afferent, uniting in the heart, upward-flowing, governing the brain– we don't need to be running an ego program. We can live in the sensing. We can locate identity in the living embodied flux of feeling. The mind can fall silent and we are still here. This is why the Lakhota language has no word for 'me.'

Thinking, in the sense of cognition, rumination, a river of dialog, self-talk, turns on when we leave this location, or when we are forced out. Thinking turns on when we shift out of ventral vagal into defense.

Thinking turns on when we are not able to reside in the embodied feeling. When, in our autonomic analogy of water, liquid water turns to steam.

Thinking is what happens when we get kicked out of the body, when it doesn't feel good in here, when the neuroception shifts from safety to danger.

Thinking is what happens when we grow up unsafe.

Do you understand the degree to which our experience of who we are is governed by our lack of safety?

Most of us have attached our sense of who we are to the inside of the cage we pulled back into because it wasn't safe to open our hearts out into the world.

Most of who (and what) most of us hang our identity on is the residue of a habit of contraction forced upon us by exposure to environments–familial, social, cultural–where we cannot be who we actually are because it is not safe. If we cannot be who we actually are, then we do not know who we actually are.

If we are not safe we pull back like snails, drawn inward. Ego is the sense-making and self-talk of the self we experience pulled back inside our own defensive perimeter.

That contraction, my friends, is not who you are.

Yet we are in the habit of identifying with this contraction.

⊕

At the origin of consciousness: a crime scene. Something happens–some catastrophe. Some inciting incident; something goes horribly awry. There is a rupture. All of our ordinary ways of coping–everything we have learned thus far, are inadequate to respond. We enter a space of liminality where we no longer know the rules, where nothing is fixed, where nothing makes sense. A sort of between-the-worlds. Mary Watkins and Helene Shulman, in *Toward Psychologies of Liberation*, remind us that Gloria Anzaldúa, in describing this, uses the Nahuatl word:

*nepantla.*

## Nepantla (nahuatl): the in-between-ness

This upending, be it the psychedelic experience of an early hominid ancestor on the plains, following in the wake of the herd, who pops a handful of small mushrooms in her mouth as she is walking, and some half hour later, discovers herself tilting into a novel perceptual landscape, a strange concatenation of sudden sensation, vividness, waves of color, the seeming solidity of the world melting down, something entirely unknown arising, the mind grappling to steady itself...or be it the tear in the fabric of the non-dual, the sudden withdrawal into defense that grants an edge to the body...are related, these phenomena. Crime scenes. Moments when our worlds fall apart.

*Turning and turning in the widening gyre*

*The falcon cannot hear the falconer;*

*Things fall apart; the centre cannot hold;*

*Mere anarchy is loosed upon the world*

It is necessary. That's what I'm trying to tell you. This is how awareness is born. It's not the crime that is the awareness. The crime is the wound, the inciting incident, that makes it necessary to grow the awareness. Consciousness is the alteration of structure required to stanch the bleeding.

The crime is the wound, the inciting incident, that makes it necessary to grow the awareness. Awareness is not the mushroom. Awareness is the faculty required to not go crazy when the mushroom dissolves the world.

This is important. Because if it is the mushroom, you'll have to keep eating the mushroom again and again and again. But if it is the faculty–you can grow the faculty. The faculty you can take with you. It is *portable*. Grow that faculty and life herself becomes the magical catalyst. You don't have to keep tripping balls to evolve. You just have to learn how to not grow crazy when life dissolves your world.

My crime scene, seven years old, the Ryder truck, everything

I love receding from view. The garden in the past, exile ahead. This is the inciting incident. This is the cross I will bear, my particular originating wound, what I will grapple with for 35 years, what will set the cardinal direction of my life's quest for meaning. The wound necessitates the awakening. It is an initiatory process. The traumatic injury is necessary foreground to the post-traumatic growth. The deepest teacher cuts you to the bone.

The crisis sets the banquet table. Can we eat it? Metabolize it without going mad? Let it make us mad and then grow a new self large enough to become sane again?

Is it not like this each time we grow into a bigger worldview? A wider field of awareness? I don't know anyone who does this willingly. Who would choose apocalypse? Who would choose to have their meaning-making system collapse? And yet, somehow, isn't it through the world ending that the new world begins?

Birth is a catastrophe with a marvelous outcome. The feotal ejection reflex–what pushes the baby out–is a massive dose of cortisol that creates a crisis we can't think our way out of. Creates a crisis that can only be overcome through utter transformation. A crisis so great that it gives birth not merely to the baby, but to the mother and the father. A crisis that breaks worlds open: one so great that it can only be overcome by love.

Another way of saying all of this: the crime scene is cortisol. Is danger, is threat, is stress, is trauma. Who we are becoming is on the other side of that. Who we are becoming is the kind of love we have to grow to knit ourselves a broader version of ourselves; one large enough to include the wound from that crime scene. A version of Self broad enough to include the collapse, the breakdown, the apocalypse.

There are two verb-based flows here: a deathing and a birthing. Things fall apart, we have to overcome them in order to put ourselves back together.

This is initiatory. Transformation always holds the very real possibility of madness and death. If you are going to transform your mind, you could lose it. Psycho-pathology is, in part, those who have been incompletely or improperly initiated. Crime with no ensuing rebirth.

This is why the sages say–don't resist the river. The river is bigger than you are, it is stronger than you are. We are not in control. It is also why the sages say: don't get your psychedelics in the mail. It's not the mushroom. It's the faculty required to not go crazy. And when the stakes are that high–do you really want to go that alone? Or would it not be wiser to have an experienced community of support?

Is it possible to open to the inward apocalypse? It's a tall order, but if we recognize that the crime scene is the doorway?

And yet, study it we must. This particular wound that happens to each of us. What are its specific signatures. By what doorway did the apocalypse enter? What is its essence? What is the inciting incident? We must study it so keenly that we develop a new faculty of awareness: the faculty.

Anzaldúa again: *La faculdad*: the ability to receive the depth of the world and soulfulness by breaking through habitual modes of relating to reality and perceiving consciousness. La faculdad does not reside in reason but in the body. It is born not out of choice but out of the necessity to survive. Here we are, broadly speaking, money hoarders at the end of the world. The inciting incidents are all around us. We are tripping over them. This weekend my bank is in the process of collapsing. Democracy is ripping apart and being actively dismantled. Extinction events abound. The time is ripe for the next stage of becoming. She is brewing around us. The cauldron boiling fervently before us. Can you knit a broader version of yourself large enough to include all the catastrophe without shutting down? It's called theory of mind, but it should be called theory of heart. A secret: that's what has to grow big enough to include the end of the world.

## 09

# Sense-making on the Verge of Collapse

⊕

> *This is the way the world ends*
> *This is the way the world ends*
> *This is the way the world ends*
> *Not with a bang but a whimper*
>
> –TS Eliot, The Hollow Men

On March 9, 2023, after a fairly classic bank run, Silicon Valley Bank (SVB) collapsed and went into federal receivership.

On April 28, 2023, the US Treasury's official fiscal data website declares the national debt to be $31,458,014,678,320. For those not well versed in decimal placeholders, that is thirty-one trillion, four hundred and fifty eight billion, fourteen million, six hundred and seventy two thousand, three hundred and twenty dollars. A million is a thousand thousands. A billion is a thousand millions. A trillion is a thousand billions. So 31.45 thousand billions. At the time of this writing, the federal government is debating how to raise the debt ceiling, which they have hit, in order to permit them to make this number larger. Neither side here is interested in compromise. The US government runs out of money June 5, 2023. Interesting times.

On December 31, 2022, SVB held $152 billion in uninsured deposits. These were deposits that exceeded the FDIC cap of $250,000 per account. As the federal reserve raised rates, and capital conditions tightened, many of the startups SVB banked experienced increases in their funding costs as debt became more expensive, in tandem with significant valuation contraction because many of them are pre-revenue, which caused them to need to withdraw more cash, putting increasing deposit outflow pressure on the bank. In tandem, the bank's book of loans was losing value due to interest rate hikes. When forced to sell $21 billion in securities to fortify their cash position, this resulted in a $1.8 billion loss, in the wake of which the bank talked about raising funds, and severely bungled a communication with customers, which is what set off the run. Hindsight being 20/20, the banks risks had begun perhaps years earlier, but of the collapse, these were the immediately proximal inciting events.

During the run, SVB's venture capital customers, who were the very people SVB had helped make incredibly wealthy, directed their portfolio companies to withdraw all funds from the bank at once. This community, which is tightly connected online, acted in a herd-like fashion, led by the one-and-only Peter Thiel: brilliant, gay, obscenely wealthy, libertarian, vindictive, and a prepper. This stampede of withdrawals led to a $40 billion deposit outflow from the bank in one day. The events that triggered the collapse, namely a $1.8 billion loss, and poor communication, which shook depositor trust, created conditions that the US government and Federal Reserve believed created systemic risk in the US banking system, at which point the federal government stepped in and took the bank into receivership. At the moment the bank went into receivership, the catalysing event at SVB, namely a $1.8 billion loss, represented .00006 percent of the federal deficit (less than one one-hundredth of one percent).

What is money? I confess that I don't understand it that well. I'm looking at a jar of coins sitting on my breakfast table as I write this, which has been sitting there for some months. It is on its way, at least theoretically, to the bank to be turned into dollars, because we don't want to walk around with our pockets filled with coins. They are too heavy and awkward a medium of exchange. This jar holds the spare parts of dollars that have been broken up, from the purchase of some odd item, that landed in someone's pocket, a shirt, jeans, the inside pocket of a jacket, my wife's purse, and were then rounded up and consolidated there. They are made of copper and nickel and were, at some point, made of silver, though no longer. But money isn't the metal, is it? Its value isn't the coin, though once, when we were on a gold standard, it was. On the coin itself, and on every dollar bill, is stamped the Great Seal of the United States.

The value of a dollar isn't in the paper. The bill, like all fiat currency, is actually a contract backed by the US government.

The same government with 31.45 trillion dollars in debt. Fiat currency is a contract tied to a worldview embodied in a nation-state. The US government is 31.45 trillion dollars in debt, which makes it by far the largest debtor on earth. The US dollar is also the reserve currency of the world.

Apple, which makes the computer I am typing this on, is the largest company in the world by market cap. This morning, that market cap stands at 2.665 trillion. But that market cap is about thirty times their earnings, which were nearly $100 billion in 2022, so the amount of money flowing through the company is a fraction of that market cap. Apple's total debt is $121 billion dollars, which is about half of one percent of the US government's total debt.

The US government isn't a company, but its debt is 260X the debt of the largest company in the world. This government had to step in to stabilizing a company whose implosion was set off by a $1.8 billion hole in their books, because in their estimation not doing so risked destabilizing the entire US banking sector.

Since the US dollar is the reserve currency of the world, and the US government is 31.45 trillion dollars in debt, and systemic risk to the US banking system can be set off by a 1.8 billion hole in a modestly sized US bank's books (as of December 31, 2022, it was the 16th largest US bank), what kind of interventions globally has, and will, the United States government make, and need to make, when and if events in other nation-states act in a manner that might destabilize this hegemony? Can you separate the foreign policy interventions of the United States from its economic interests? In the interests of who, and of what, does the United States therefore intervene? Is its interest primarily in democratic institutions and norms, or, as the largest debt-leveraged entity on earth, and in the history of the world, could there perhaps be other interventional motives?

Stay with me here, I'm still setting the table. Dinner isn't even served yet. I'll tell you when the first course is coming.

⊕

Have you ever experienced an avalanche? I started to write 'witnessed', but that word implies some kind of attending to that is outside of being impacted. I don't think it is possible to witness an avalanche. If you can see it, you will feel it.

At the present time, we have recorded a record snowpack in the Sierra. At Mammoth Mountain, in California, this winter we recorded 702 inches of snowfall. There are 12 inches in a foot. From January to March of 2023 there were a series of historic atmospheric rivers. This one particular meteorological outpost has, as a result, recorded 58 feet of snow. The interesting thing about an avalanche, and I suppose we can only use the word interesting, rather than terrifying, if we are not down-mountain of it, is that what sets it off is generally not a large event. In chaos theory, and systems dynamics these amplification effects are often called Butterfly effects. The classic metaphor is that of a butterfly's wingbeats causing a hurricane. This is a way of speaking about massive amplification loops cascading through a complex system. The snowpack is dynamic. At nearly sixty feet thick it is incredibly heavy. The compressive forces down at the bottom are tremendous. It is not uniformly dense, as different snows of different consistency have been sunned by different warmths, and melted differentially. This entire mass, of inconsistent texture and density is also stacked on hillsides, mounded at acute angles. The sun warms it, night cools it. There are layers and layers of accumulation. In these places, much of the backcountry is closed to humans. It is much too dangerous. But an avalanche, which destabilizes the entire snowpack, can be set off by a mouse.

Sixty feet of snow, thirty one trillion in debt. SVB is a mouse, treading across a snowpack in the Sierra. All it is trying to do is get home with the seeds in its mouth. Let's pause right here. The mouse is a creature in a context, an ecology. Does it have a deep understanding of this context? Does it know what it is walking on? If it did, would it walk more carefully, place its weight more judiciously? Should it have to? This is, after all, where it lives. It's not doing anything wrong. SVB was a highly-risk taking mouse. That was, in fact, part of what had made it so successful. Its cousin, First Republic, is a highly-risk averse mouse. Both of them are traversing the snowpack, like all the mice. Many of the other mice are somewhere on the risk continuum between SVB and First Republic. The most risk-taking bank, the most conservative bank. Most of them hold significant loans on commercial real estate, which, up until recently, was not a particularly risky exposure, but now, post-pandemic in a world where people don't spend their days at the office, is.

⊕

I've been a customer of First Republic for twenty-one years. First Republic is a highly-risk averse mouse. They are so risk-averse, in fact, that the average credit score in their book of mortgages is 790. I don't know what you have to do to get a credit score of 790– but let me tell you, folks, it is not living like the average American. A credit score like that means you never miss a payment on anything. You've never paid your phone bill late. Never gotten a credit card delinquent. In order to have a score that high, you have to also use the right amount of debt. What is the right amount? The amount that the banks find most advantageous. If you don't leverage yourself enough, you won't get a score that high. Too much leverage? That drops the score as well. So these people, these 790s? They are really proficient at playing by the rules of money. Individually they represent almost no credit risk. They are not going to default on a mortgage. Ok. Let's serve the first course.

## PART TWO:
## Birthing and Deathing

Ask anyone on the day they are born, and if they could answer you they would tell you that the world began that day. Ask anyone on the day they die, and if they could answer, they would tell you the world is ending that day.

Worlds begin and end all of the time. We co-inhabit a pluriverse of worlds, plunge wittingly or unwittingly through fractality. Step on a garden slug and a slug-world just ended. There is an idiomatic expression in Spanish that acknowledges: *Cada cabeza es un mundo*. Every head is a world. Birthing and deathing is the inhale and the exhale of the cosmos.

There are also, it seems, times when worlds begin and end more broadly. T.S. Eliot, writing the Hollow Men, a quote from which began this essay series, was writing in 1925 about post-war World War One Europe after the Treaty of Versailles. Many worlds ended during the first world war, as it is known at this moment in history, and many more would end during the second.

You can go to sleep in one age of the world, and wake up in the next. With complex systems, disruptive feedback patterns occur. A trend-line begins to accumulate, momentum begins to build. Often, from within the frame of reference of a system like this, the building of feedback momentum is experienced as increasing volatility. But from within the system it is difficult to perceive what may be happening, because our horizon is constrained by being within the system. It is hard to meaning-make of the patterns of waves in the ocean if you are in the ocean. You feel the waves rising and falling, and you trust the waves. You learn to surf. As the waves get bigger your technique has to evolve. It's different surfing at Lindemar State Beach, where the wave is three to eight feet hight, than at Mavericks, where it is forty. A wave that is twice as tall is four times as forceful. Amplitude increases non-linearly. Volatility compounds exponentially.

A better vantage might be had if you could step out of the ocean, behold it from some other point of view. From a different vantage point, the structure of the waves beneath the waves you were rising and falling on might be visible. If you could step out of the ocean and look at it you might notice that the waves we are experiencing are riding on something deeper that is collapsing. That the volatility is an indicator of this. If you could see that something was collapsing under the ocean of capital you might want to get out of the ocean before you got caught in a truly massive wave. A tidal wave. An avalanche.

I was born into this capitalist system, which has never really made sense to me, sometimes to my detriment. Confessionally I will share with you that my preferred relationship with money is to not have to think about it at all. I like it when it is there when I need it and otherwise not a factor. As the Founder and CEO of a company, that is not a luxury I've had for the past five years, and because I am accountable to stakeholders, and take this fiduciary responsibility very seriously, I've spent a great deal of time grappling with money. I confess, again, for how pervasive it is within the fabric of the experienced reality of modern people, I have not encountered much clear consensus about what it actually is, even among people I know who have lots of it.

Let me explain what I mean by that. I was educated, more or less by the culture at large, because my specific family did not have a particularly pragmatic approach for communicating this to me, that I should get an education, so that I could go to college, so that I could go to graduate school, so that I should go into a profession that I found interesting and challenging, get paid well, buy a house, raise a family, and repeat. As a younger person, this logic, although I saw it playing out all around me, held little appeal. The first of many problems that I had with it was that I had no idea, at 19 years old, how I wanted to spend my life, which made it hard for me to choose a major in college, which I conceptualized as the first foreclosing of options in the direction of a wide-open future that I could not yet see. This was one of many reasons, though not the most important reason, why I dropped out of school. A more important reason, tangential here, but which I have written about broadly elsewhere, is that I could not feel my own heart. If you can't feel your own heart, it's probably unwise to make a decision about how you will spend the rest of your life, but again, I'm writing all this thirty years later, more or less, and wouldn't have been able to put this into words at the time. I ended up dropping out of Yale College, in a pretty messy way, but that's another story. At the time I was deeply ashamed of this, but again in hindsight it was the right decision. I stepped out of the map of any known future that had been written for me, and there began the journey that has brought me to today. I note the significance of the line, from that first major rupture with an expected future, to where I stand now.

When I dropped out of school, at nineteen, I found myself somewhat accidentally at odds with the received narrative of what you should be doing in this modern neoliberal capitalist world, which has a habit of refracting being(ness) through the lens of what is useful to capital. What the neoliberal world would like you to do is 'become a productive citizen', which means having a credit score of 790, like my fellow customers at First Republic Bank. From my perspective at the time, how could I consent to eventually trading my time for money, if I didn't know what I was going to be doing with that time? It is perhaps generally unwise to trade something you cherish (time) for something you don't understand (money).

So, back to First Republic Bank, which, if you don't know this yet, has collapsed.

I need you to understand why it matters that First Republic collapsed, or at least why I think it matters, an event which took place on May 1, 2023. Since I don't believe in accidents, I want to speak with you for a moment about the celestial import of that specific day. May 1, 2023 occurred during an eclipse gateway, which is a moment on earth between two eclipses, in this case a solar eclipse on April 20, at the new moon, and a lunar eclipse on May 5, at the full moon. An eclipse gateway introduces a pattern of energy into the earthplane, the physics of which, in plain language, generate the possibility of novel frequencies of becoming, and then surface what must be transformed in order to arrive at them. May 1, in addition, is also Beltane cross quarter day, which, again without going too far into the Celtic calendar, is halfway between the spring equinox and the summer solstice, and the beginning of summer. Let us summarize by calling it a day with non-trivial celestial alignments, in a larger process of the possibilities of new energies arriving.

First Republic, and I think this is important to say, didn't really do anything wrong. Their troubles began around the same time as Silicon Valley Bank, when they were identified as having similar risk exposures, e.g., a disproportionately high percentage of accounts beyond the $250,000 FDIC limits of insurance. Yet that is where the similarities ended. On March 9, the day SVB collapsed, I had spoken to a stakeholder in my own company who advised me to pull all of my money from First Republic. What are you talking about? I asked him. He explained that he was in contact with venture capital funds who were doing that themselves, to the tune of 50 and 60 million dollars in withdrawals apiece.

What happened to First Republic, rather suddenly, was that their business model put them underwater. Since they were highly risk-averse, how did this happen? Principally this is because the macro-economic environment changed as the Federal

Reserve altered monetary policy by raising interest rates. Let me put this more bluntly. The seaside estate in Hawaii worth $50 million? Only so if it is not underwater. The Fed is the ocean in this case. It raised, on purpose, the sea-level 10 feet in 12 months. Suddenly the most desirable properties in the world were underwater. I am speaking metaphorically here, but I'm also not. I am speaking polyphorically. The Fed, $31.45 trillion in debt, changed the ocean. The largest active agent, with the most to lose, suddenly changed the rules. Suddenly, on purpose, pushed the level of the ocean up onto land to protect other larger interests of itself, i.e., quelling inflation. Sea levels are rising, but the sea levels of what world? The economic world?

Capitalism is a self-terminating algorithm based on socializing costs to the many while privatizing gain for the few. Etch that sentence, courtesy of Alnoor Ladha and Lynn Murphy, into your mind. Carve it into consciousness and the headboard of your bed, and you won't be surprised by what is coming down the road for all of us. The few can be the owners of capital. The few can also be the interests of the reserve currency of the world.

Now ask yourself, what is narcissism?

Narcissism is a self-terminating algorithm based on socializing costs to the many while privatizing gain for the narcissist.

Do you see a resemblance? Does capitalism give birth to narcissism? Yes. Does narcissism give birth to capitalism? Yes. Fractality again. One at the level of the entire global operating system, the other at the level of the individual egoic operating system. Both contractions designed to avoid relationship.

⊕

I am aware that any telling of this will leave out something necessary, and yet I need to tell this story, which is also not about the bank, but about something more personal. It is connected to the bank, fractally, because I'm interested in a pattern here: the pattern of collapse.

But I'm interested also in the relationship between the global operating system (neoliberal capitalism) and the individual operating system (psyche), and the way that they reinforce and stand in for one another.

I'm interested in the phenomenon of collapse at both of these levels of system, and I'm interested in what is on the other side of collapse. Through the door of collapse. The spiritual utility of collapse to bring us back to the ground.

Most people will never walk through the door of collapse, because the collapse itself will be so intolerable to their system that they will freak out. Unable to compute, reason, or sense-make beyond the edge of this known, they will either internally combust (suicidally) or externally combust (homicidally). If you take the temperature of the mental health of modern humans, which, in my day job, I get to do globally in nearly 50 countries, you will perceive that this is happening with alarmingly accelerating frequency right now.

Yet what if collapse, the zero point itself, is actually a form of deep medicine? What if it is a gateway to the next world? What if, like ego dissolution on psychedelics, the experience of death is just the falling away of something that isn't really you anyway?

Systems collapse how come? Houses collapse how come? Economies collapse how come? Psyches collapse how come?

Any structure that collapses, at some level does so because it is unable to resist the load of structural forces bearing in upon it. In the realm of the economic, these structural forces are debt. It was realization of debt that collapsed SVB, and then, gradually

First Republic. With SVB this happened almost immediately, a spectacular implosion. With First Republic, the bank teetered, for some time, like a prize fighter caught off-guard by an uppercut. It was not obvious that the bank would necessarily fall. But the blows kept raining down, in a kind of delayed reaction, the bad news kept coming, the short sellers kept stomping, and eventually it succumbed to the pressure.

I have endured the collapse of a mind, and although the pressures were not debt, but the collapse of other supporting structures, and extreme stress, the outcome was more or less the same.

If something collapses, it was not, by definition, resilient. What is resilience? We could say that it is the ability to continue to maintain stability under increasing structural forces.

⊕

The story I want to tell is about my own zero point, which occurred on May 4, three days after the collapse of First Republic. I note the parallel with the bank, and I note the time proximity, but strangely I did not collapse.

⊕

In order to write this, I am going to have to employ a method imported from trauma healing, and trauma narratives. At the heart of this story is moment that I will refer to as time zero. Time zero occurred on Thursday May 4 at approximately 10 am PST. I was sitting in my car, a blue Tesla, which was out of charge, and which I had just unsuccessfully attempted to attach to four charging ports in a row. The car had, nominally, zero miles of range left. I was in the driver's seat, phone in hand, trying to get the charging app to work when I checked my bank accounts. At that moment both my personal and business banking accounts hit zero.

I stopped, set down the phone, and took a deep breath.

⊕

For that moment, time zero, to make sense, in the context of the trajectory of my broader life, and not simply a series of essays about financial collapse, I need to incorporate another moment, which is somehow the opposite or the inversion of a zero point, which I'll call a birthing point. By the logic of that awareness, which occurs to me in this moment, the time zero that I am referring to above would be a deathing point. They are very different, yet related.

The deathing point, time zero, was the moment that foreclosed a set of possibilities, or awakened me suddenly from a set of ensphering illusions in which I have spent my entire life up to this point. That I did not experience this as a danger to my self, my person, in any more fundamental way, but was able to experience and pass through it, without flinching, was in no small part due to the birthing point that preceeded it, which occurred at about 3 pm PST on Monday, May 1, the same day that my bank collapsed.

It was also due, more remotely, to my mind having collapsed in 2012, and my having rebuilt it over six years on a much firmer foundation, although this again is another story.

I had, that afternoon of May 1, taken a walk with a new friend in Sonoma, for the purposes of clarifying my mind with respect to an on-going negotiation with a client in which I was then enmeshed, and had been at that point for 9 continuous days. At this moment, the birthing moment, I felt, in a specific embodied way, with complete relaxation and total clarity, the essential shape of the next incarnation of my purpose in this lifetime.

This happened so fully, crisply, vibrationally, and completely that I stopped to take a photograph of what I was looking at, sitting in her living room, and announced, a propos of nothing, "I have just been born into the next incarnation of my purpose."

Together we ate cake, which I happened to have brought, apparently for such an occasion, which I didn't know would happen when I bought it in a bakery on the town square.

⊕

I am the Founder and CEO of a company that was, on paper, according to the person holding our interim Chief Financial role, who is certified in the valuation of such entities, worth 100 million USD.

The company has developed a set of novel modalities for treating stress-related disorders through a diagnostic taxonomy that centers autonomic physiology in the treatment of dis-ease, and a deep learning software, of which I am the principal architect. This understanding of physiology is married to an understanding of ancestral awareness practice.

Over the past 18 months we have stood on the threshold of three partnerships. The first, with a celebrated impact investment firm funded by a billionaire enterpreneur, would have put $10 million into the company.

The second, with the Stanford University School of Medicine, would have taught our work to the medical faculty of that institution.

The third, with a celebrated Executive coaching and leadership development firm, would have partnered with them to create a version of our software platform tailored for leadership, and implemented it with executives in companies and organizations around the world including Fortune 100 companies and NATO.

The least mysterious dissolution of one of these prospective partnerships happened when the institution we were considering partnering with attempted to steal our work. In both other cases, the first, and the last, what ended up getting in the way was harder to understand.

Since I am, by all medical accounts, supposed to be dead, and since the reason I am not dead is partly that I have learned to trust and follow parts of own intrinsic intuitional and spiritual guidance system that the english language does not have words for, because it doesn't recognize that they exist, in each of these cases I have made the decision not through cognition, but because there was some part of my innate sovereign knowing that refused.

It was the same in the most recent case, the finalization of which happened at about 5:30 am PST on May 4, 3.5 hours before time zero.

At that time I sent an email to the 25 people who had been in some way engaged in our negotiations alerting them to our withdrawal.

In the moment before sending this email, I had stepped outside my back door to consult with Nature about this action. It was before dawn and the sky was still dark. As I turned my attention prayerfully heavenward, a shooting star cross-cut the sky above me in a bloom of yellow fire and winked out.

I walked inside and hit send.

In the previous four months, I had worked almost exclusively on this project. For the two months preceding its ending, it was all the work I did. Until the day the project collapsed I was as certain as you can be of anything that it would complete. Our time value of money calculations, based on figures that our prospective partner had provided us, had given us a net benefit of $17 million in revenue over five years as the worst possible outcome of the agreement. The scenarios that seemed more likely were in the $50 to $100 million ballpark. Because of this, I had not made backup financial plans.

⊕

On Thursday May 4, 2023, at 10:05 am, sitting in my car, I stepped out of capitalism. Maybe I failed out of it, maybe I graduated out of it, maybe I vomited it up, maybe it vomited me up. But suddenly, in that moment, I set it down.

It fell away, like something behind me. I crossed an internal threshold. I cannot explain it fully, nor will I attempt here to try. I was as if some psychic armature cleaved, or dissolved, or was no longer bearing weight.

I experienced a strange sense of liberation. The direction of gravity altered somewhat.

I found myself in a new land.

Things were both the same, and not the same. I found myself feeling very grounded, and disoriented. It was a little bit like I felt when it became clear, in 2016, that Donald J. Trump had been elected President, though less horrifying. The direction of gravity simply changed.

I got out of the car, which was also at zero and wouldn't go anywhere anyway, and walked back to my house.

⊕

How do we know, in a moment, whether we are coming together or falling apart? I've had dissolution experiences, psychic collapses, but they were generally gated by terror. This was not that. Something broke. I crossed a threshold, but I did not falter, and there was no eccentricity in the system: I didn't go spinning off wildly, freaking into the ether, untethered, crashing into outer dark.

Rather I realized, very soberly, that there was no capitalist saviour coming: an investor, an institution, a partner. That the organization's debt was sitting squarely on my shoulders, and that while modest by early technology company standards was not small by comparison to an individual.

⊕

I was indoctrinated into a school of entrepreneurship, partly by the intent of my business mentors, partly by the climate of Silicon Valley, and the macro-economic climate that pervaded for many years, to be comfortable with large numbers - equity and debt - as fairly abstract.

In the sudden brilliance of time zero, with the spotlight of capitalism removed, both the false light of extraordinary returns, and the real risk of my family's exposure became clear to me, hard and concrete.

The deal an entrepreneur makes, in the worldview inspired by Silicon Valley, is to trade extraordinary effort and risk for the possibility of extraordinary reward. This is the calculus of the start-up world.

What I saw at one level was that I did not need the extraordinary reward, and could no longer take the extraordinary risk.

⊕

I want to save you some trouble here, because I do not recommend that you try this at home. I do not recommend that I tried this at home. I didn't get to this moment by choice. I got there because I didn't want to sell out the work I have spent nearly 30 years giving birthing. I was able to endure the moment, I believe, because somewhere along the line of Founding and CEO'ing a company I became convinced that I was wealthy, which is not the same as having cash. Being rich is what you can see of someone's wealth, but being wealthy is what you cannot see.

If I was another person, in another life–if I didn't have the firm conviction that we had created something of utility to humanity–if under any other circumstances, and probably if this event had happened to me even a day previous, I wouldn't have been able to endure it. I think I would have felt very afraid.

But I did not feel afraid for some reason. Partly it was that I didn't feel I had made an error, done anything wrong. I did not have regret.

Partly, I suppose, it was that the magnitude of the moment became quite real for me and my competitive survival instinct rose up because my family itself was on the line, and I leaned in. I would end up working for the next 17 days in a row, a minimum of 12 hours each day, in order to re-stabilize the company. This would put at 34 days in a row the number I had worked since beginning to negotiate the deal we withdrew from. The event, this zero point, mobilized extremely large amounts of survival energy. It was not without impact, and I was not unaware, as it was happening, how high the stakes were for my family.

And yet, strangely, I didn't contract. I sat there, breathing, at time zero, feeling my feet on the ground and experiencing the strange reality that I had zero dollars in the world.

When I say this, I want to be clear that I do not mean I had zero dollars in my checking account. I had zero dollars period. Everything I had ever earned and saved I had already invested in my company. The condominium my wife and I had owned as an investment property for our retirement we had sold and invested in the company. I had tapped out every credit card, every line of credit including a personal line at our bank, and a home equity line. I mean zero. I'm not fucking around.

The past two years had been like this. My company had raised about half a million dollars, and my wife and I had invested the same. I had contributed four years of work without taking a salary, taken on business debt (not included in the calculus above), used COVID to funnel mortgage reductions into the business (shhh), etc. We kept having these grand *almosts*, as I've detailed above. Almost the billionaire impact investors, almost Stanford University School of Medicine, and now almost this.

There was, simply, no more wiggle room. No investor to call for a loan–we had done that the month before. It was, simply, zero.

Zero. Nothing. Emptiness. In my car with zero miles of range. That's where I was.

⊕

What do you do in a moment like this?

⊕

I considered, very carefully, bankrupting the company. Was there a way to just step back, to let it fall? We had about fifty investors who would go to zero. By far the largest was myself. If I chose this, what would I do next? The thought came: I would do the same thing I had been doing, but with another legal shell. And in the process? Zero everyone, including myself, who had put faith in us, and create a huge legal and logistical headache. This probability receded.

What if I faced the emergence/ emergency directly?

What would that look like?

What would it mean to drop out of capitalism, to let it fall away?

What thoughtforms would I have to abandon? What would I have to let go of? What levers, what controls would I have to stop striving for?

What would a post capitalist lens, and a post capitalist landscape dictate?

What is money?

What is sovereignty?

How to survive on the other side of collapse?

⊕

This exit, what I am calling time zero, happens on the 14th day of negotiating. It is May 4th. The previous time I have had a day off was April 16.

⊕

I am tracking coordinates of possibility toward the emergence of a future I cannot clearly see yet. The momentum and coordinating metaphor for our work is that of a giant tree. It is rooted in what we understand.

During this phase, for the following several weeks, I will kick out experiments, and these will be like limbs that we grow out of the main body of the tree. Some of them will be healthy, some of them will break off. Some of them we will outgrow as the apical tip of the tree moves north, and it re-prioritizes the distribution of resources.

I am sense-making in the dark, tracking based on senses I do not understand, listening for a vitality I am somewhat afraid to claim a right to- a villaging instinct.

That faith I bring to this process, and it is rightly faith, is that if we stay with the taproot of the small band hunter gatherer ethics, and their expression, they will lead us into a clearing in the forest.

⊕

Now another continuous fourteen days after May 4, I realize, in the shower this morning, that I have worked 32 consecutive days. It occurs to me, as a thought, that the last time I worked this many days, at this intensity, without stopping, was during a war. Suddenly, unbidden, standing under the stream of water, I am standing in the midst of a battle. I am standing on a small promontory, and there are men fighting all around me, hand-to-hand. I am just a little bit higher up, but the colors, the brightness of their garments, red fabric fluttering, the sounds of battle, the smell of the sea, all of these reach me. I swim to the surface again, and the image passes.

Towelling off I think of the seeds in the forest that will not sprout without wildfire. They need that focused heat to crack them open, to become who they are meant to be.

Later that same morning I am on the road to the land, the dirt road in the last quarter mile, thinking about my neighbor as I pass. This thought, a reflex of disgust, distrust, and anger, causes me to accelerate, without thinking about it, and despite the fact that I suddenly see it stretched out in the road, sunning itself, I am unable to stop quickly enough to avoid running over the snake. It is large, stretched out, and I screech to a stop some thirty feet beyond it, suck in my breath.

I do not like killing animals. I do not like running things over. I hit a beautiful jackrabbit once, that leapt out of the bushes right in front of my car, and setting its limp body to the side of the road was something I felt all the way through me. I get out of the car, and approach it, and a hawk calls overhead. The creature is wounded, lying in the road, a section of its guts spilling out near the tail. It is clearly stunned, and I find myself trying to figure out the most compassionate way to deal with it. Could it survive? Suddenly, on approach, I notice the diamond pattern on its back, the flared shape of the head, and I realize it is venomous. I notice, in this moment, the rattle.

I walk back to my car, where, in the trunk, I have a small axe. I return to the snake, and in one motion drop down and sever it cleanly in two. The head and top third of the body flip over, the pale yellow-white of its underside, and movement ceases.

I pick up the head–I want it to study for some reason, and I carry it back to my car. The body is soft, smooth, drapes over my hand. The skin almost velvety, extraordinarily supple, soft. This takes me by surprise. I am very careful to avoid the mouth. The rear seats are down because I'm carrying lumber, and I set it belly-side up on the seatback, drive the rest of the way to the land, unlock the gate, and unload the lumber. When this is done, about ten minutes later, I am staring at the neck of the creature, the understructure of its jaw, when it suddenly flips over and begins to writhe.

This astonishes me. I use a metal rod to knock it off the seat onto the ground, and I study it. How on earth? Two thirds of its body are gone- there is a gaping chasm opening ten inches behind the head, I can see into the inner chamber of its body, but it is unmistakeably alive now, coiled into an S-shape, eyes wide open. I am fully focused on it now, monitoring my own body sensations and the eeriness of all of this.

I return to the trunk, pick up the axe again, and I kill the snake a second time. This time I sever the head two inches behind the skull in a graceful curve of the neck. Both sections of the body still, but I am unnerved. I take the axe, and I walk back out the driveway, shirtless, and up the road. I am moving with intensity. It occurs to me that anyone who happened to drive up the road would find me striding, barechested, brandishing an axe. The smell of dust kicks off, the heat of the sun. It is silent except for the occasional scrabble of a squirrel through the trees, the scree of a jay. I walk all the way back to the limp body stretched out in the road, kneel down, and sever the rattle from the body. I pick this up, and study it, the carotenous structure almost like some mutant finger nail, shaped like a seed pod, layered on itself. I take the rattle and walk back to the head. These twins- the skull and the rattle I set on a board while I deliberate.

There is something talismanic in this trophy. I'm not a collector of the spoils of war, but it is not lost on me me that my day dawned with the rememberance of a battle in a previous incarnation. Something is moving through me. What is the lesson of all of this?

I determine that the appropriate course of action is to find a box, something significant, to contain the elemental parts of this creature that I have beheaded. It occurs to me that I should wear it, on my person, somehow. This I ponder, as I set the head and rattle into a glass box in my car.

On the drive home I call me friend who is a *murakame*: one who sees. Wanna hear an interesting story? I ask him. As we are talking he scans the internet, and discovers that a snake's heart and lungs are close to the head. This explains the resurrection. Venomous snakes represent betrayal, he tells me.

When you cut off the enemy, cut it off as close to the head as possible- this is the moral, the import of the story I walk out of the day with. I thought it was dead, and it came back to life, this venomous creature.

What does it represent? What do I have to cut off? What have I cut off? What is the venomous head?

I study it throughout the day. There is something of the head of the medusa about it, something dragon-like. The eyes are still wide-open. By squeezing the back of the head the jaws open and the fangs eject. Beneath each fang, the wide scimitar of each, there is, slender nearly as a hair, a nearly invisible needle. With the head clenched in my right hand, its mouth forced open, the fangs articulated, I ponder the deadliness contained in the fierce arrowhead of this creature's skull.

⊕

Who betrays? It's hard for me, sometimes, to believe that I was born into a civilization that is trying to kill me.

But the learning of this lifetime is just that. It won't be the obvious fangs either– the fangs of debt, or stress, it probably won't be random violence, or a slow death from pollution. It will be the shadow that delivers the poison, a needle seemingly innocuous as a hair.

I am talking about the worldview itself, and the way that it smuggles itself across the borders of the psyche because it lives at the very thresholds where the psyche shifts into defense. It lives in the interstices of the tower walls of the fortress that the ego erects when we feel danger. In the delicate seductive lie that by accumulating more we'll be safer. And it slips in, like a mist, ethereal, when the boundaries dissolve, telling us that if we could just more securely enclose we would be ok.

It exists because we haven't been able to remember, coherently, what came before, and we haven't been able to imagine, coherently, what exists beyond.

It exists because men, fearful of the power of women, fearful of that which gives birth, its proximity to the life-force herself, blamed our mother, the first mother, our earthly mother, for their experience of alienation, and proceeded to subjugate the feminine, the intuitive, the holistic, our own right brains, in fact, to the masculine, linear, and logical.

Here, on the continent I call my home, its unique flavor was the intentional mis-representation of the beauty and mystery of night, of dark, of deepest blackness, its transmogrification from mystery into evil. It was the displacement of white evil onto dark bodies, and the body supremacy elaborated from that.

And this needle of venom, this injection was also the uprooting from the ground, our seduction, like the legions of Rome turning eyes toward the conquering sun, that taught us to turn our attention uniquely heavenward, as the daily worship of the elemental was culled, the rise and fall of seasons, the tightening of winter, its chastening and fearful cold that pushes our attention inward, brings us close to the earth and the hearth, whispers stories of deprivation and trues our devotion, close round the fire, to simply surviving together.

Of the spring, the first crocuses poking through snow, ice, the melt of snow from the mountains, the rushing of springs, the sudden vault in the step of the deer, the lengthening grass, the return of the sun, the increase of abundance, the sweetness of May, the ripening of cherries, the speaking of vows. The longest day, the sun's radiance, the sweat of the brow. The ripening of the babe in the womb, the corn in the field, the song of the crickets, the slow exhalation of heat off the land. The meteor showers of August, the work preparing for harvest. The table set, hands held, the village circled. The blessing of abundance. The peak of the foliage, the forest aflame, the gathering beauty of night. These ways of knowing that come up through the feet cut off, and the people who live cthonically, earth-worshippingly, genocided.

And so it crowds in on us, this default, secreting itself into the cracks and fissures of the mind, this death mask whose form is legion, alien, face-grabbing.

I have the rattlesnake's head on my desk now, in a box. Even now, boiled down to skull only, it still reeks of death. You might think it morbid, but I want to remember that there's a death cult here all around us, fangs drawn.

I am a grandson of witches who did not burn, and I have come back to destory the empire, to awaken you from the trance.

10

# Sam Altman Went to My Highschool

⊕

RESPONDING TO NEWS ITEMS FROM FRIDAY, November 17 to Wednesday November 22, 2023, in The New York Times, beginning with:

*OpenAI's Board Pushes Out Sam Altman, Its High-Profile C.E.O.*

and concluding with

*Sam Altman Is Reinstated as OpenAI's Chief Executive*

AND ARTICLES, PODCASTS, AND COMMENTARIES RELATED THERETO.

Sam Altman (was/is) a Co-Founder and CEO of OpenAI, the unusual San Francisco non-profit/capped for-profit startup at the center of the generative AI (boom)(hype)(event horizon).

## BACKGROUND

For the past year, since ChatGPT was released to the general public on November 30, 2022, there has been an explosion around generative AI. The amount of capital that has flooded into the space since that time, which includes not merely investments made by Microsoft on the order of 10 billion USD, nor an increase in the valuation of AI chipmaker Nvidia on the order of nearly two trillion USD (and these are not the only capital flows, to be clear), are being accompanied by what is essentially an arms race (self-described by the companies themselves) between the behemoths of tech (Google, Meta, Microsoft, Empire Musk) over shaping the future of this technology. (Last year the future was the meta-verse, this year it is AI. How quickly we seize on the next big thing; how quickly we forget the last.)

Silicon Valley, which is prone to grand pronouncements, has declared in its techno-optimism that one day we will merge with silicon, and this hybrid of human and machine will usher in a golden age of humanity. Like all good zealots, the faithful speak with missionary zeal about the rapture of this possibility, while pointing out, to assure us of their rectitude, that they are taking seriously the risks that such technology also could annihilate us in myriad absurd ways, including turning everything into paperclips. In this ambiguity between expiatory and apocalyptic outcomes, seduced by the possibility of endless profits, fearful of existential risks, we cannot look away. We are entranced.

Many serious and otherwise quite 'rational' people speak in hushed and rapturous tones about the development of a kind of super-intelligence that is being created, or could be: an Artificial General Intelligence that would exceed all of the intelligences of the human brain and either lead us to general glory or annihilate us. While many of these people are avowed atheists, dare I point out here that the structure of this thoughtform, though directed toward a silicon creation of our own design, i.e., Artificial, is identical to that of earlier hominids talking about other forms of super-intelligence? Indigenous forms of super-intelligence, as it were? What does it say about us, modern humans, that we have filtered this quest for divine or demonic reflection through silicon narcissism?

At the center of this end-stage capitalism cultural phenomenon is a single organization, OpenAI, which has accreted an astonishing array of the capital and engineering talent in this technical area, and has launched the buzziest products underpinning generative AI (including ChatGPT), and at the center of this organization a single charismatic leader, Sam Altman, who was lauded universally in Silicon Valley as a sort of wunderkind until he was unceremoniously deposed on November 17, 2023 as the CEO of the organization he founded by the non-profit board of that self-same organization, which, unlike most boards did not have a fiduciary duty to shareholders, employees, or the company itself, but rather under the terms of OpenAI's governing charter, whose "primary fiduciary duty is to humanity."

The board, in announcing the firing of Altman, found that the CEO, "was not consistently candid in his communications with the board, hindering its ability to exercise its responsibilities." Not consistently candid in his communications means, in its most generous and benign interpretation, that he was not honest and forthright.

Until, now, apparently, five days later, in the wake of an enormous pressure campaign and a company-wide revolt, he is no longer deposed.

In this article I would like to bring to our attention some aspects of the current spectacle that I feel are not being adequately noticed.

ARGUMENT

Amidst the general polarizing clamor of Artificial Intelligence (is it the devil's rocketship or the salvatio of humanity?) what sometimes gets lost in my humble opinion is the reality that modern humans are an Artificial Intelligence.

I make this assertion because, vis-a-vis the Living World, in which we are embedded, the cosmological and teleological view of modernity is fundamentally a death cult: it destroys the only biosphere in the known universe, on the daily, with the same alacrity that we eat breakfast cereal. Said slightly differently: every time you start your car you take a shit in your mother's mouth.

We have, as modern humans, deviated foundationally from the Original Instructions to steward and live in harmony with all of Life: to guard and serve and protect it. And so, I propose to you that rather than calling the current silicon animations Artificial Intelligence, we ought to recognize that they are twice artificial: the orphaned children of orphaned children. Exponentially artificial. Artificial squared. Twice exiled.

## 2AI

I will refer to them in this essay, therefore, as twice Artificial Intelligence: thus, 2AI. We, modern humans cosmologically derivative of the Cartesian dictum *I think therefore I am*, are already AI. Small band hunter gatherers (sbhg) are the baseline of human normalcy.[1] They are not Artificial Intelligence, but simply Intelligence. Original intelligence, non-deviated from the Original Instructions. So as not to confuse you, gentle reader, I will denote this II, rather than I. Indigenous Intelligence. So arrayed therefore before us are 2AI, AI, and II.

2AI (silicon), AI (moderns), II (sbhg)

Before I deepen into and sharpen this argument, which I will shortly do, I would like to point out to you, to get this out of the way, that as a training circumstance– a world of ensphering data– the internet is largely a toilet. A child, silicon or carbon-based, whose ersatz brain is some kind of neural network, learns the world by interacting with it, and if you understand how a large language model gets built, either in a human or in a computer, you understand that the 'data' you are feeding it gets modeled into its structure, whether cellular or silicon. E.g., through Hebbian Learning 'Neurons that fire together wire together.' (Large Language Models are computational neural networks.)

Were I, abstractly speaking, designing a nutritional curriculum for my toddler, be she human or silicon, I would feed her the internet with about as much likelihood as I would have my own child drink and eat what she found in the toilet. Step back far

---

1 See Narvaez, Darcia, *Neurobiology and the Development of Human Morality*, WW Norton, New York, (2014).

enough and you can see, pretty clearly, that although it contains also the words and works of Gandhi, Martin Luther King Junior, Shakespeare, celestial spheres, and a non-trivial bit of the numinous, the primary gist of the internet is pornography, cat videos, selfies, and conspiracy theories. I don't let my teenager free-range on the internet, any more than I would have a clown car of carnival barkers teach my toddler to talk, and she has the human sensibilities and guardrails that come from being raised within the ethics of a family, an extended tribal family, that has given her a bottom-up grounding in embodied morality. The silicon 2AIs birthed by Sam Altman and his ilk are being assembled by hoovering up vast mountains of toilet. They have no such moral groundedness. We moderns are exiled intelligences building silicon beasts fed on foraged shit and illegally scraped copyrighted material[2], and which are therefore fairly likely to be as batshit crazy as any kid whose primary caloric intake was sourced from a commode.

Sam Altman went to my highschool. He graduated about ten years after me, and I do not know him personally, but I know something about the milieu in which he came of age, as I have some embodied familiarity with what he means when he said, to an interviewer from the New York magazine, "I am a midwestern Jew from an awkward childhood at best, to say it very politely." I am likewise a person of Jewish ancestry from the midwest with an awkward childhood who went to that self-same school. We had childhoods that were awkward in different ways, and we ended up at the school, which was an elite college preparatory, 7th through 12th grade, for different reasons, and with different reasons for being outsiders, yet both, in our own ways, confronted the parochial, conservative, satisfied, and affluent midwestern gaze normalized by an elite institution in a provincial city. I know something about the ambition it kindled, at a level that felt feral, like an allergic reaction (or a survival response) in me.

---

2 September 20, 2023: *Franzen, Grisham and Other Prominent Authors Sue OpenAI* The suit, filed with the Authors Guild, accuses the A.I. company of infringing on authors' copyrights, claiming it used their books to train its ChatGPT chatbot.

December 27, 2023: *The Times Sues OpenAI and Microsoft Over A.I. Use of Copyrighted Work*: Millions of articles from The New York Times were used to train chatbots that now compete with it, the lawsuit said.

This was, in part, an ambition fueled by being on the outward end of an intimately exclusionary gaze, intimately proximate with levers of power I could not touch, and although this would manifest in life choices completely different from Mr. Altman's, it would fuel my own iconoclastic nature, and conduct me to the leftward edge of California, which is the edge of the country you head for if you have interesting ideas and a family name that opens no doors.[3]

I spent several decades after highschool in fear–an existential fear even, like terror in the furnace of the belly fear–of feeling I would not be capable of leaving the kind of mark on the world I felt I needed to in order to redeem myself in the eyes of those I had been surrounded by, during adolescence, who had contributed to making me feel so small, and so alone. Strip away all of the pretense and shame of this, the ambition that was a reaction to the terror at its center, and at its core was the fear that I would never feel ok about myself.

I'm not comparing myself to Mr. Altman, I'm simply noticing something about the context in which both of us spent our adolescence in St. Louis, and what I know it did to me. Our highschool was an odd place. In my graduating class of 93 students, there were 47 National Merit Semi-Finalists, if memory does not err (these are folks who scored in the 99th percentile of the pre-college enterance exams I believe). The drive to stand out, the drive to be seen, and for me the drive to have sovereignty over the shape of my own future stood out, in highschool, because I found myself downstream of structures of power I stood outside of, was subject to, and could not influence. My outsider status was partly a function of class, Altman's was of sexuality. Yet there is something about being an outsider that kindles a fire in the belly.

People for whom the status quo is really working don't generally start revolutions.

As an outsider, you sometimes learn not to care very much about what other people think of you, because it is too painful. This

---

3   I have noticed that when you meet people on the East Coast, and they are trying to place you they want to know who your family is, and in St. Louis people ask you where you went to highschool.

tends to migrate your compass for action inward. To move the locus of control more deeply inside. Many of the innovations in my own work (in Autonomics) have come from actively disregarding what the field-at-large was saying about a given issue. You learn to follow your own inward directive.

One final thing, of which I am aware. Midwestern Jewish boys are often doted on by their mothers in a particular way. This can give us a level of confidence that if not tempered by enough failure and rejection to cool the steel can blossom into messianic delusion.[4]

And so, a kind of loose algorithm: I propose Mr. Altman's present state was forged by = intrinsic aptitude x unearned confidence x outsider status x furnace in the belly x disregard for what others think x messianic delusion.

Altman Algorithm:

Intrinsic aptitude x unearned confidence x outsider status x furance in the belly x disregard for what others think x messianic delusion = Motivational Trajectory

It wouldn't hold up as math, but I think it identifies some of the primary variables you are going to see play out.

About Mr. Altman, in the same article in New York magazine, a friend in his inner circle described him to the interviewer as "the most ambitious person I know who is still *sane* [emphasis mine], and I know 20,000 people in Silicon Valley."

ALIENATION

---

4  If your mother tells you, enough times, that you are God's gift to the world, you might start to believe it. From the New York magazine profile: "*If you weren't raised in a midwestern middle-class Jewish family — and I say this from experience — it's hard to imagine the latent self-confidence such a family can instill in a son.* "One of the very best things my parents did for me was constant (multiple times a day, I think?) affirmations of their love and belief that I could do anything," Jack Altman [Sam's brother] has said. The stores of confidence that result are fantastical, narcotic, weapons grade. They're like an extra valve in your heart."

The principal problem I have with 2AI is modern humans. By which I mean alienation. By which I mean that the people who are making these silicon beasts, irrespective of their beneficent intent, which let's say for the present moment I am not calling into question, are already themselves operating from exile in ways that they do not understand. Modern humans have already deviated from the ancestral baseline in connection and relatedness that undergirds 99% of our lineage history, which is why we find ourselves in the hot mess, the poly-crisis, of a world on fire. What I am saying is that I do not trust a cabal of 38-year old hyper-rich wunderkinds, howsoever quote unquote intelligent they may be, peering into the mytho-poetic mirror of silicon, fueled by the fever-dream of unhinged capital and power, and self-acknowledgingly aware of their own traumatic histories [e.g., from an awkward childhood at best, to say it very politely], while concomitantly unaware of how these histories are baked into their worldviews like yeast is baked into bread, to generate second order intelligences that are not even more alienated than they do not know they are.

What this means, I imagine, is that we are presently instantiating psychopathology in silicon in ways that will be difficult to remove, and will have complicated and unforeseen adverse imperial consequences. This is why the New York magazine article I am referring to calls Altman the Oppenheimer of this age.

Someone with training in autonomic physiology, moral reasoning, and generative artificial intelligence please correct me if I'm wrong, but my layperson's understanding of a Large Language Model (LLM), which is what OpenAI has been developing, and which has been deployed in ChatGPT, for example, is that it doesn't have a heart. And the heart is what is required to properly (e.g., non-alienatingly) organize the mind.

So, here's the problem. I'm simplifying here, but in 2014, Darcia Narvaez, PhD, Professor Emerita, and a trans-disciplinary researcher in psychology at the University of Notre Dame published the astounding *Neurobiology and the Development of Human Morality,* which up-ended the field of moral reasoning by proposing, explaining, and documenting how morality is built, bottom-up, by the embodied experience of safety and relatedness children do, or do not have, in the evolved nest of culture. Her thesis, distilled, is based on the recognition that our lineage history as hominids emerges from the ancestral cultural background of having lived, for 99% of our lineage history, in small band hunter gatherer kin groups. These groups, which were deeply egalitarian, nomadic (we were seasonally following the migratory paths of animals), and embedded in the orienting rhythmicity of the Living World, consistently engaged in 9 infant and childrearing practices[5] that gave mothers and infants, and then growing children, the proper neural inputs of safety and relatedness required to build human beings that are intrinsically moral. This ancestral baseline was, for most of our evolutionary history, implicit to culture, and therefore not documented per se. About 12,000 years ago, with the dawn of agriculture, human populations attained surplus food for the first time. This was, I am proposing, the dawn of the age of AI, as it led rapidly to a series of innovations in abstraction, generating numeracy and literacy, birthing property boundaries and right angles, initiating the multi-generational transfer of property, and rapidly initiating a re-organization of human sociability from horizontal modes of relatedness to vertical modes of domination.

Speaking again in distillate, we could chart this deviation from the ancestral baseline in the movement of the locus of identity from the heart to the head. We moved from animistic relating in a warmly horizontal world of *the felt*, to abstract dominating in a coldly vertical world of *the thought*. This is when our intelligence began to become artificial: this deviation from the ancestral baseline.

Modern civilization, so-called, is the tragic story of how we became exiled from who we really are. This exile is such a de facto part of the experience of modern life, written into the origin stories of western civilization, inscribed in the founding documents

---

5  Provisioned by a community and not simply by mothers, the evolved nest for young children includes (Hewlett and Lamb, 2005; Narvaez and Bradshaw, 2023): (1) soothing perinatal experiences; (2) breastfeeding on request for several years; (3) nearly constant positive touch; (4) appropriate responses to keep baby optimally aroused; (5) multiple allomothers (care by responsive individuals other than mothers such as fathers and grandmothers); (6) multiage self-directed free play; and (7) social embeddedness, with a positive, welcoming social climate, and (8) nature immersion, and (9) healing practices.

of European thoughtform-derived identity, from the story of the Fall, which blames our predicament of exile on a woman and a snake (clearly written by men, this is a story that blames the current (notionally fallen) world on a woman and the creature with its belly on the ground who stands in for the Indigenous), to the Homeric Odyssey, which tells the story of that man skilled in all ways of contending, who has been orphaned by war, and is trying to make his way home. (*The Odyssey* yields, most fruitfully, to an interpretation as the psychodrama of healing a traumatic stress injury.) Yet we cannot seem to get the camera pulled back wide enough (western civilization, aka AI, did not start two or three thousand years ago, but more like twelve thousand), to see the rupture. AI begins with the axial shift from horizontal relating (the kinship worldview) to vertical thinking (the domination paradigm).

Strangely, modernity knows that it is lost. It is conscious of being exiled. It knows it has become unmoored, and this is nowhere in greater evidence than in the breadth and depth of illbeing plaguing us, the host of stress-related disorders and traumatic injuries that swarm about us like a cloud of flies. It just doesn't know how to heal this.

Cutting through all of this to my argument here, with clean blade, 2AI is derivative of this level of baseline alienation. 2AI is derivative of AI, algorithmically. What Darcia comes elucidating, through her trans-disciplinary synthesis, is that the creation of morality, when it happens, is not an intellectual act, as it had been rated by European philosophy, but an embodied dance of relationality informed by a child's experience of deep safety, giving rise to the experience of kinship with all of Life. This is an education– in the Latinate sense of the word, *educare* (to draw forth)– of the heart. It is not a cognitive values schema.

I am moral (if I am) because I feel connected. (To myself, to others, to the Living World.) When I feel connected, I have a relationship, when I have a relationship I care about that to which I feel connected. What I care about I take care of. e.g., I express morality towards.

At a biological level, this morality, which is a verb, is mediated by a neuro-physiological system that I like to call the Connection

System. The center of your connection system is your heart. In order for this system to turn on, and for it to assume its proper (e.g., sovereign) and correct place in your life, such that it can generate your ongoing experience of kinship, which births wellbeing, it must be nourished by safety and connection. When this happens regularly enough, this system runs your brain. I am not speaking metaphorically. It literally generates the wavestate in the heart, at 1.618 Hz, the heartrate variability of the Golden Mean or Fibonacci sequence, that platforms your cognition. You will recognize it, because it is how nature is designed.

Part of what I am trying to explain to you is that when you are well, your brain is downstream of your heart. This is why Indigenous people say that the farthest journey most humans will ever make is traversing the 18 inches from the head to the heart. The heart is the home of humans who are well.

Modern humans, ensphered by threat, birthed into millenia of exile, denatured by empire, are generally not running this system as their physiological baseline. This is why, at a physiological level, I am calling modern humans AI. When we begin to more fully instantiate, occupy, and baseline the Connection System– to embody it– we come home to ourselves, beginning to make the endogenous transition from AI to II. We re-indigenize our physiologies. Through safety, which opens the door to connection, which opens the door to interoception, which opens the door to non-cognitive ways of knowing, we open the portals to relatedness that can convey us back into the experience of kinship that is the wellspring of enduring wellbeing. We return the heart to its proper central and sovereign place running our minds. This occurs through the circuits of sociability. Human (social mammal) wellbeing is relational – social – in nature. Part of what I am saying to you is that your mind is not your brain.

Your brain is not even your brain, if by brain you mean the organ that knows what we know. Your brain is your entire body. And all of you is required to be moral. From the skin in. Your skin is the outer surface of your brain. Your interoceptive awareness is the felt domain of your moral compass. A Large Language Model without a body is an aberration. This is not a form of intelligence. It is alienation squared.

With this in mind it is important to understand that most of the people in Silicon Valley who are building the technologies, so-called, of the modern world, do not understand it this way at all, are locked in their heads, and are not good at being either in their bodies or in relationship. Our communications systems, the ones that have scaled–the ones our kids are addicted to– from Facebook to the social network formally known as Twitter, to the makers of the new AI are being built by people who are, for the most part, diagnostically emotionally inexpressive, nearly off the charts in terms of what Sam Altman's sister Annie calls, *"Just the lack of fucks given."* They are not good at being in relationships, and they do not care that they are not good at being in relationships.

Elon Musk co-founded OpenAI, as a nonprofit, with Altman and four others in 2015. In 2021, he hosted Saturday Night Live, and in his opening monologue, which you can and should watch, because it explains a lot about what is happening in technology in our world at present, told everyone watching that he has Asperger's Syndrome. I sent this video, which is about 5 minutes long, to Stephen Porges, PhD, the Developer of the Polyvagal Theory and the world's leading expert on the relationship between the Autonomic Nervous System and behavior, asking for his opinion about what he saw. Musk is, during the monologue, clearly nervous, and there are a number of moments when the way that he is standing, his head and neck movements, the way his head and neck relate to his torso, his posture, gesture, and articulation were expressive of motor movement patterns I found deeply and clinically unusual. Porges' response was a single sentence. What he said was, *"That man co-regulates with objects."*

What did he mean? What I understand Steve to be saying is that what he could see, in the video, was that the places in the room Musk is looking, the way that he is finding safety, the elements of the space to which he is relating, are not people, but things. Objects. This is understandable for someone who is nervous, but peculiar because the room is full of humans. It is Saturday Night LIVE.

THAT'S BECAUSE I DON'T ALWAYS
HAVE A LOT OF INTONATION OR

And yet this is important for us all to understand. Musk is a preternaturally brilliant architect of objects: cars, spaceships, etc., because he is relating primary with *things*, not *people*. Said slightly differently: If you were an artist, and your lover was a robot, you'd design a beautiful robot. This is the story of Pygmalion and Galatea: it's not new.

To a fairly extreme degree, and increasingly so, our 'technology leaders' are abstract heads carried around by bodies, cognition-forward, and non-human-relating. This is both the byproduct of alienation, and invites the causal replication of it in the systems such leaders design. I submit the social network formerly known as Twitter as evidence in this regard.

We can make all kinds of things out of silicon. But until we heal our own hearts, until we are no longer ourselves AI, until we are no longer alienated, we cannot help but make children, silicon or otherwise, who are also and likewise alienated.

This is not an essay about Sam Altman really, or whether or not he should lead OpenAI, or whether or not the board of the organization made a good decision, or why such a decision was made. This is an essay about something deeper, about what it means to be alienated, and how it seems that we have built silicon half-brains by looking in the mirror and seeing our modern selves, and thinking they are somehow whole, when in fact they are an alienated imitation of something already alienated.

From the perspective of the Original Fire, what we are building, twice removed from intelligence, does not seem, in its current incarnation, likely to help bring us home.

# 11

# Oracular Dream

In the dream, which occurs the night of a full moon, I am visiting my godfather in his apartment in New York, though it is not his apartment in New York as I remember it. I cannot seem to remember the beginning of the dream. The part that I remember begins with me talking to him in a sort of living room, elegant, slightly antique by way of furnishings. The apartment seems to have marble floors, I am guessing, and the kind of light haze of dust that comes in a building not from being dirty but simply from being old. From a prior era. As if time is moving at a different rate, the rate of postal mail, the rate of memory that stretches back millenia, an accumulation of history, et cetera. The dust of ink settling off the printed page, old newspapers slowly decomposing, the smell of ancient books. To the extent that I remember it, the lighting in the apartment seems to have been coming from lamps, seems to create small pools of illumination. There are no windows in the room, no evidence of sun or moonlight, of the outside world. There is a stillness, no ambient noise beyond our voices, yet the quiet is not oppressive. I don't realize until after the dream is done, and I have awakened, that the apartment is in Rome.

He is a film director and producer in his mid-seventies, my godfather. Accomplished, literature, debonair, celebrated. We haven't spent a great deal of time together face-to-face, but I have known him since I was a very small child. He was a writer then. His career inclined into film criticism, and then he began to write movies. Some of which have been quite famously received. There are pictures of him at Cannes, red carpets, et cetera. As I moved into my forties and became more estranged from my father, I have found myself reaching out to him more often. He has adult children whom I have the general impression he speaks to infrequently. Are we surrogate family for one another, to some extent? Bound by care, long familiarity, literary inclination, shared interests? We speak on the phone, sometimes at length, every couple of months. Sometimes when I am driving.

I find it reassuring. Perhaps he does as well.

In the dream we are in his apartment, he seems to be getting ready to go somewhere, and we are talking. It is unclear what time of day it is. Maybe he is putting on a watch. It seems likely he is wearing a shirt that is well tailored, and he might be buttoning or unbuttoning the cuffs. His voice has, has always had, a sort of melodic timbre that is pleasing to the ear and this time is no different. A voice you'd like to hear clearly, stand closer to, make sure you catch the inflection of each word. Maybe he is gathering some papers together while we speak. There is the general sense that he is getting ready, perhaps to meet someone for dinner, but things are unhurried. There is no rush.

At some point Sam Altman, the CEO of OpenAI, shows up in the apartment. It grows awkward because he does not acknowledge me and I find myself talking to him at increasingly close range, attempting to get his attention.

My godfather, I realize as I write this, reflecting on the dream, is part of the writers union, which has just been involved in a strike in part about AI. He has, for many years, been intimately involved in these negotiations. The New York Times has recently sued AI and Microsoft over copyright infringement. But there Sam is in my godfather's apartment, and if he doesn't know Sam my godfather is non-chalant about his presence. At the time, in the dream, as it is unfolding, it is my assumption that Sam is there because my godfather invited him, why else would he be there? But now I'm not so sure. I'm no longer so sure what the dream was about, though from within it I did not experience disorientation. During the dream I assumed the apartment was in New York, but by the end of the dream, and you'll see why in a second, I am sure it was in Rome, though I didn't realize this, viscerally, until I was awake.

It is strange to have a dream, a dream that might be in some fashion oracular, or a fragment of knowing, or intuiting, and then to realize later, in a waking state, holding the dream up to examine it, like an unfamiliar artifact, turning it this way and that way in the light, holding it up to waking examination, that I didn't understand the dream as it was happening. That it wasn't for me, that I was not the protagonist. That though the dream happened as if in my mind, that my involvement might have been peripheral. I do not realize this until much later.

In the dream I am standing four, then three, then two feet away from Sam talking to him and he does not respond but is rather preoccupied by something in his hands. Not as obvious as a Rubik's cube, but something. Something that captures his attention, captivates. The dream is not overt. The sense is of his attention otherwise engaged. I am unable to get his attention even standing close enough to him that he has to move around me and this odd dance proceeds for a couple of steps... I'm trying to tell him we went to the same highschool. His body is moving around me, has to step back and to the side, but I haven't seemed to reach his attention. It is elsewhere.

*We went to the same highschool. Burroughs. In St. Louis,* I'm saying.

He never fully looks up. I use a canned line, a line I wrote in an essay about him, trying to break through, trying to get his attention. In the dream, even as I say it I feel I am throwing myself at his feet, and am faintly disgusted by that, even then.

*We are both Jews from an awkward childhood that went to Burroughs.* I say this to break through to him, though it's not entirely true, my Jewishness very provisional, ancestral to be sure, but embodied very little, very little a part of my identity, my sense of self. It feels obsequious when I say it, fawning, but I'm trying to get his attention, pull him up out of whatever occupies him. This all happens pretty fast.

I can't remember if he is speaking to my godfather. I assumed in the dream that they were talking, perhaps they were. Yet now, when I attempt to recall it, I cannot remember.

When I say this last bit about childhood he looks up, fleetingly, for just a split-second. Some tiny hint of recognition.

And then we are leaving, out the door, and here is where the dream grows fluidly weird, he is standing on the stairs outside the apartment, and he is holding the end of a rope that has attached to the door of my godfather's apartment, my godfather the celebrated film writer, director, and producer, and the rope is somewhat elastic and Sam is leaning all of his weight on the rope, holding the door shut– he is neither strong nor unathletic, and the whole thing in the dream has the tenor of a joke, and yet my godfather cannot get out of the apartment because Sam has attached a rope to the door and is holding it closed with his body weight.

And there is this feeling, this energy in the dream of, *Oh, isn't Sam a clever prankster, a jolly sort of troublemaker*, as if my godfather is the one who is saying this, or acknowledging it, where else might this sense be coming from?, its not coming from Sam, who is waifish and yet intent, somehow, holding this elastic rope. Elfish and yet focused, no?

And afterwards I think– perhaps I should have helped with the rope? Assisted my godfather to get out? But no, in the dream it didn't even occur to me. Rather, in the dream, my attention is diverted by the grandeur of the foyer, the internal landing of the building, the sculptural architecture of which is notably sublime, a sort of red marble I am guessing engraved with ornament, finials, scrollery, a level of artistic excellence so high, so sublime, that I somehow forget about Sam, who is getting in the elevator... in the dream I imagine with my godfather, I'm still under the impression that they are going somewhere together, though I never see my godfather leave the apartment. To dinner?

And my attention is brought to the inward architecture of the edifice, and I begin to walk down the staircase, and the floor below is grander than the one we are on, the staircase continues down, in a rectangular spiraling descent, sections moving straight, turning 90 degrees to the left, and proceeding. On the next floor down is a larger internal area in the building, almost a lobby, there is a restaurant, waiters in tuxedos maybe, other elegant people, but my attention is riveted on the sculptural detail. (I have attempted to carve stone, I have some sense of the process, I know how much effort this level of workmanship requires, the mallet first, the chisels, then chisels with teeth, finer and finer, then the sanding, finer and finer, like polishing glass, to achieve this luster).

The staircase widens, and– this really gets my attention– there are a series of small sculpted heads, white now, translucent almost, Carrera marble? Statuario? Or something with more yellow, slightly more waxy...of animals. Dogs. Just the heads, sitting with some regular periodicity on the steps. Maybe sculptured heads of other animals as well. Marble heads of dogs, their artisanship so intricate, so astonishing that I kneel down– there are people walking to and fro, waiters carrying trays, I kneel down to have a look, I touch this talismanic object, why are there sculpted dog's heads sitting at intervals on the stairs where anyone could kick them over?

I keep descending, though maybe by the time I have kneeled to examine the dog's head I am three or four stories down from where I started. The apartment was on the 8th floor, somehow I know this.

I keep descending. The building getting wider inside, opening into a sort of atrium. There are more people.

And then I am in the lobby, walking across, pushing out of the building through a set of glass doors, there is a sort of bazaar in front of the building, furniture, a very long - thirty foot - couch for sale, some of it quite nice yet not as elegant as what is inside, a sort of marketplace, I am now on the street, there is noise of the city. My godfather and Sam long gone, disgorged by the elevator some time ago I imagine, perhaps while I was kneeling. Yet I didn't see this. Don't in fact know where either one has got to.

And as I leave the building I realize– the petrol fumes, the pigeons, the fashion, the hue of the sunlight– not New York, but Rome.

As if.

As if the building itself is the very edifice of civilization. As if the floors are not height, not verticality, but time...

As if I am moving back through history, but a history embedded into the present moment, culminating with it, me in an apartment on the 8th floor with my godfather, this point in the history of the world, writing a story, writing history, and the Oracle of AI has appeared, uninvited, and attempted to shut the storyteller in.

I don't realize this, don't understand it fully, until right now.

## 12

# Automatities of Sacrifice Among Inadvertent Members of the Death Cult

⊕

In this essay, I would like to unite themes that I classify broadly under the rubric of 'we do not understand where our wellbeing comes from' with themes of denaturing self-sacrifice required of prisoners of the death cult, e.g., modernity, whereby individuals will ritually and of their own free will sacrifice their wellbeing out of self-complicity with death structures of which they are consciously (mentally) unaware, and viscerally (in an embodied manner) lucidly aware.

This self-sacrifice, which is normative and socially validated, e.g., *"I'm killing myself at work,"* and similar such formulations, is actually attended a certain status by both the person making the sacrifice, and the broader normalizing gaze. This is to say that it is attended with a badge of honor until it actually kills the person, or renders them incapable of working (e.g., medical or mental health collapse), at which point ritualized forms of regret and remorse take effect, with concomitant wonderings about how this happened, or was allowed to happen, and token affirmations that people would be served by better work-life balance, or 'self-care', both notions that have been weaponized and inverted by domination mind, and displace the critical gaze from the carceral systems (death cult/ predation systems) themselves to the individual victims (prey) thereof.

I have noted elsewhere in this volume that the death cult, like any self-perpetuating system, seeks to elevate functionaries who serve it well. Because the cult itself is pathogenic, necrogenic (to be precise), death-creating and death-birthing, it will elevate functionaries who are more skilled death technicians, many of whom, unaware of the overarching structure, goals, and function of the cult serve it self-sacrificingly in exchange for localized material (extractive) gain. The promises of the cult, which I am proposing extend as a meta- and micro-localized textural fabric of domination (a carceral archipelago, to use Foucault's phrase) pervading the modern social order, are that by serving it, you will achieve, for your localized family (e.g., those within the sphere of your immediate protection) great material benefits (e.g., wealth and security), by extracting from some Commons (of resources, ideas, etc.). This extraction is configured, by the cult, as a form of intelligence or acumen, and rewarded with material wealth. The particulars of this arrangement, vis-a-vis sector (e.g., chemical, fossil fuel, mining, agriculture, education, non-profit, etc.), industry, mechanism of extraction (i.e., are we extracting resources, labor, attention, time, etc.) are irrelevant, as the foundation pattern is the same.

Functionaries adept in the maximization of extraction are considered nominally virtuous, good, effective (within the realm of the system, company, organization, etc.), and thereby elevated in the systems: they get promoted, their agendas and techniques get advanced. The localized determinations of what constitutes effectiveness, the means thereby, etc., are localized and culturally-bound (e.g., what is permissible ethically to effectuate extraction – i.e., making people work longer hours or breaking people's kneecaps), but the ends are the same, e.g., greater extractive yield.

In Michel Foucault's formulations on the structuring of relations of power, he presents the Panopticon, a prison architecture proposed by the Utilitarian philosopher Jeremy Bentham, as an image of modern society. Within the Panopticon, the prisoners are locked in individual cells, which are arranged inside a circular structure at the center of which is a guard tower (central vantage point). From the guard tower in the center, the prisoners can be seen at all times. The knowledge of their visibility, ie., the degree to which they are aware of constantly being surveilled, eventually induces them to monitor and regulate their own actions. As the gaze of surveillance is turned upon oneself, self-scrutiny to return one to normative behavioral choices becomes the most potent form of social control.

Part of Foucault's insight into the construction of power relations is to articulate that power does not reside simply with the state, or with an institution (or set of institutions), but is rather distributed. Within the image of a carceral archipelago, Foucault uses the metaphor of a group of interrelated islands to represent *"the way in which a form of punitive system is physically dispersed yet at the same time covers the entirety of society"* (Foucault, 1980b, 68). Foucault conceptualized the Panopticon as a sort of template for all forms of social control, and saw society increasingly as a carceral system. (His prison, my death cult.)

Modern social life, he noted, in the 1970s, long before 'Artificial Intelligences' began to move unmonitored and untrammeled through the social spaces of the Internet, hoovering up vast mountains of personal data without permission, and assembling them into machine geographies of abstract mind deployable for carceral objectives, was becoming increasingly a system of surveillance, self-surveillance, and social control. Foucault's notion of panopticism highlights the systematic ordering, controlling, recording, differentiating, and comparing of an entire society through both visible and invisible forces. These forces are deployed to control, modify, torture, mark, and train bodies to perform, carry out tasks, and behave in particular ways without the need for overt coercive measures (Foucault, 1977, 25–6).

The strands of this that I would like to differentiate, are the notional constructions of what is 'good or virtuous' with respect to the maintenance of the death cult, from notions of what is 'good and virtuous' with respect to what is necessary to preserve and maintain life, because the territorial collision of these notionalities is now playing out across the landscapes of our bodies with increasing violence as we move deeper into the realities of systemic collapse.

I want to localize this inquiry to the body, to the felt sense, and to symptoms and symptomology of illbeing, because this is the purview and domain of my expertise, and because in my clinical practice and teaching I am working with and receiving patients and clients who are formulating illbeing in particularly medicalized manners when in fact, from my perspective, their bodies are functionally disclosing the territorial collision between the innate embodied quest for vitality and aliveness that the mammalian body expresses, with the carceral system structured through domination, expressed through thoughtforms of compliance, and subjugating the body. This conflict, in many of the people I am treating, expresses in dis-ease.

If you want to understand the polycrisis of the modern world: the degree to which our modalities of extractive domination intersect the biotic necessities of life, you don't need to look further than the individual body. It is not even necessary to extend the gaze to the global climate crisis or totalizing war. The war is playing out across the landscape of the individual psyche: the battleground is the body.

It is playing out in the symptoms and forms of illbeing of the modern world. It is playing out in auto-immune and inflammatory disease, gastro-intestinal disorders, stress-related disorders of all kinds, anxiety, depression, insomnia, heart disease. Chronic, toxic, and traumatic stress, and its normalization. As above, so below. As in macro-cosm, so in micro-cosm. The wildfires are playing out both in the boreal forests, and in your immune system: that is what I am saying. Your body is a fractal of the Mother Earth.

The battlefield of the polycrisis of modernity is your own body and wellbeing. You need look no further than that. This is because, straightforwardly, the localized experience of the death cult of modernity articulated through the carceral archipelago Foucault describes is embodied in the collective soma of the modern world, and this collective soma structures normative gravitational forces that individual bodies feel.

The sense that you have of what you should be doing, how you should be spending your time– the notional virtues required to be a 'good and responsible' citizen, a good worker, a good provider, etc., are exerting gravitational and shaping forces on your body and mind all the time.

Your mind, e.g., the locus of your thinking, has been acculturated into these normative patterns through mechanisms of socialization, which include what you've learned from your family, culture, tribe(s), friends, country, religion, media, advertising, Youtube, Tiktok, etc., – all the ensphering channels whereby the ambient information streams of culture are channeled as felt and conceptual information into the inner landscapes of your mind and body. They are also channeled through your fears, where you've been taught that there is not enough for everyone, that life in a state of nature is nasty, solitary, brutish, and short. That selfishness and competition are virtuous, etc. This constitutes, broadly, the civilizational operating system.

To the extent that you have been acculturated, without critical awareness, into the 'reality' or 'facticity' of this incoming information/ worldview, which is structured as the ambient normative cultural/civilizational field, you have been indoctrinated into a way of seeing, or understanding reality that propagates the agenda of the death cult, which is the normalized domination paradigm in which modernity is enmeshed. This paradigm originates, as I have said previously, in alienation. Its origin is Supremacy– a movement out of horizontality and relatedness as a result of separation from direct contact with the Source. Civilization so-called, modernity as we know it, is entirely downstream of this separation.

One of the things that happens, with regularity, when people first encounter, and then begin to understand our work is that they quit their jobs. Sometimes this happens quickly, and sometimes it takes 13 years.[6] What I believe is happening in these cases is that individuals are beginning to become conscious of the degree to which their own bodies have become a sacrifice zone, and that this has often happened without their permission or even awareness.

They recognize that this has happened to the degree that they are experiencing stress and or symptomology: they do not feel well. Yet as they gain the tools, practices, and conceptual distinctions for attending to the present-moment embodied experience of this sacrifice, they become less compliant to it. This has led, historically, to the paradox of institutions, organizations, and government agencies learning about our work on wellbeing, hiring us to increase wellbeing of their staff, and then seeing their staff depart. Usually, the organizations count this as a failure, but it is the opposite. People have awakened to reality of the system's structure. What had been invisibilized has become visible and they have chosen *life*.

I have said that our work consists of three things. We teach healing, sovereignty, and how to inherit our possible beauty. These are, of course, deeply related. In order to claim this sovereignty, we must become aware of the degree to which our bodies and minds are, as extensions of the territory of the death cult, already criss-crossed by networks of extractive conduit. Our bodies are already, as it were, pierced and tattooed and scarred by the pipes and pipelines that have been stuck into us to extract our vitality, our labor, and our attention, as well as the drugs required to maintain this flow. We do not ordinarily think of our jobs, or

---

6  I am aware of people quitting within weeks of training with us, and of people taking many years to fully germinate this determination. Awareness ripens at different rates in different contexts with different necessities. The timing is not ours.

social media, in this way. But within a domination paradigm, the currency of the realm is extraction, and your body, a microcosm of the earth, is this site of extraction. Your body is the mine.

And yet, and yet, because you have been extracted from for so long, because it is so normal, there are filaments and hoses running into your body that you cannot even see. That you have been trained to imagine are part of yourself. At this moment may they become visible to you, and may you awaken, with a startle, and begin to remove the apparatus of death from your Sacred and Sovereign body, that the innate vitality that is the groundstate of the Universal Force may re-weave its sovereign architecture through the map of your body, being, and becoming.

## 13

# You Ain't Jesus, Bruh

⊕

I have written at length about modernity as a death cult, and a necrogenic (death-birthing) context. I would like, in this essay, to continue elaborating some necessary distinctions around the foundation wound that gave birth to the modern era, a wound of alienation, which I have elsewhere and will here continue to call the Schizophrenia of Supremacy.

My contention is that modernity as we know it (cognitively and epistemologically) and as we viscerally experience it (ontogenically) is characterized by alienation from the Source context, which is something that shapes both our minds and something that is experienced in the body. This alienation is not merely, or even principally, an abstraction: rather it is an embodied alienation: a concretized physical and physiological lack of relatedness that we wear as an embedded and embodied feature of our daily experience. It is not a cognition, and it is not 'somewhere over there': it is, rather, existential and embodied: a hole in the grounded center of our bodies and ability to feel and know ourselves in relation to the living fabric of the Universe of which we are a part.

Modern people talk about being 'children of the Universe' but most of us FEEL like children of an angry god (relatedness through a vindictive god), or children of a tortured god (relatedness to an agonized god), or children of no god whatsoever (feeling isolated and alone), and we ACT like Children of Demons and Fossil Fuel, raping one another and the earth with the same alacrity with which we eat breakfast cereal. These perversions in relating arise from foundational and very ancient wounds.

The 'Source context' from which we have become structurally and experientially alienated is our experience of relating with All That Is, which ancestral cultures have variously characterized as 'building ropes of relatedness with all of the Creation (San people of the Kalahari) or Mitakuye Oyás'in (Lakota). (Although this is generically translated as 'All my Relations' its actual meaning is something more like: The Universe is speaking through the energy of the relationship between you and I and All Things- and therefore everything is related to All Things. See the linguistics work of Tiokasin Ghosthorse of the Cheyenne River Lakota.)

Source cultures that predate the modern, and both the San culture and the Lakota culture are several hundred thousand years old– the San culture generally acknowledged to be so, the Lakota known by the culture itself to be so– are characterized by groundedness in this original relating. Both cultures are, it bears noting, foundationally Animist.

Modernity began about 12,000 years ago. What happened sometime around then was that the way that we had been organizing society, in Small Band Hunter Gatherer groups, kin group of 25-35 members, began to drift into novel patterns of social organization. This shift seems to have taken place diasporically from the approximate location of the San people in the Kalahari, and may have been catalyzed by a number of inciting incidents. There are a pantheon of stories in the compendium of canonical origin stories of modernity, several of which have been included in the Bible, which contain resonant within them the echoes of earlier grapplings with this story, including principally in my mind the story of the expulsion of Adam and Eve from the Garden of Eden, which seems to be a documentation of our falling out of relationship with All That Is, and which was blamed on a woman (our feminine natures) and a snake (this creature with belly on the ground represents the Indigenous).

If we read the Garden of Eden as not a static place (e.g. a geographic location between the Tigris and Euphrates rivers) but rather a psychic terrain of relatedness, the story describes an inciting incident that displaced us from living in relatedness to All Things, in nakedness, which the story configures as innocence, but which is more sensibly understood as harmonization, e.g., of being part of, or One with, Nature. (Garments would be insulators from relatedness, which we did not need. We wanted all of our skin in contact with all of Nature.) The before-time in the story, the time in the Garden (capital G), was the time when humans sang their relatedness with All That Is, and heard and understood the linguistic relating (the humming of the celestial spheres, the language of the birds and the wolves, etc) and participated in it. We sang the body electric, as it were, in mutuality with all things. Our nakedness was a document to our relatedness. We wanted to touch and be touched by everything.

And then there was an accident, a tragedy, a trauma– something happens, of which we are dimly aware and in dire need of explaining, that severs our access to this original (aboriginal) state, and we are thrown out of the Garden. And this is where the Bible configures the origin of time, where the Book of Genesis begins. A fall from relating. (The Fall (capital F) from relating). A cornerstone of the modern Christian religion, as it has been configured over the millenia through a game of distortional trans-linguistic and trans-cosmological telephone since the Founder of the religion established it a couple of thousand years ago, this is known as Original Sin, which, with greater humility, we might simply see as a formulation of the problem of foundational alienation and an attempt to explain how it came about that we are divorced from the Source context.

I think it is helpful to think of the ejection from the Garden of Eden as a dismemberment. We were cut off from something, a primal umbilicus, and have since then needed a method of getting tied back to it. e.g., religion, which means, etymologically, tying back. From the Latin re-ligio. Tying (again). What we needed tying back to was/is the Source context from which we have been dislocated, or dismembered. The umbilicus of relatedness that was severed.

Aspects of being thrown out of relatedness linguistically (e.g., from an original language) are treated again in the story of the Tower of Babel, which is configured (accurately) as the result of a kind of arrogance– humans try to build a vertical tower to reach the plane of the Absolute, and as a result of this hubris lose their ability to communicate with one another in an original ur-language.

> *Now the whole world had one language and a common speech. 2 As people moved eastward,[a] they found a plain in Shinar[b] and settled there.*
>
> *3 They said to each other, "Come, let's make bricks and bake them thoroughly." They used brick instead of stone, and tar for mortar. 4 Then they said, "Come, let us build ourselves a city, with a tower that reaches to the heavens, so that we may make a name for ourselves; otherwise we will be scattered over the face of the whole earth."*
>
> *5 But the Lord came down to see the city and the tower the people were building. 6 The Lord said, "If as one people speaking the same language they have begun to do this, then nothing they plan to do will be impossible for them. 7 Come, let us go down and confuse their language so they will not understand each other."*
>
> *8 So the Lord scattered them from there over all the earth, and they stopped building the city. 9 That is why it was called Babel[c]—because there the Lord confused the language of the whole world. From there the Lord scattered them over the face of the whole earth.*
>
> *–Genesis 11:1–9*

There is, I would contend, and we will return to this, something important about the recognition, in the story, that trying to build a tower to the heavens, trying to climb upward vertically, is what got us in trouble in Babel. This movement up, away from the earth, gets us thrown down, deeper than we were before.

In trying to climb up higher (ascend vertically) we are thrown down lower (pushed into descent.) Our attempt to climb above gets parts of us forced below: gets another part of our coherence (linguistically) dismembered.

I'd like to invite you to notice that both of these stories are stories of dismemberment. They are attempts to explain successive or progressive degrees of alienation from relatedness. First from the Garden, then in language. There is a third story of dismemberment, this time with the action literalized: Cain and Abel.

Another story that contains source frequencies of this movement from Small Band Hunter Gatherer to fixed agrarian settlements and pastoral peoples (shepherding the animals) is the story of Cain and Abel, in which the offering of Cain, an offering of fruits of the soil (plants), is not looked upon by the Lord with favor:

> 3 *In the course of time Cain brought some of the fruits of the soil as an offering to the Lord. 4 And Abel also brought an offering—fat portions from some of the firstborn of his flock. The Lord looked with favor on Abel and his offering, 5 but on Cain and his offering he did not look with favor. So Cain was very angry, and his face was downcast.*
>
> *–Genesis 4:3–5*

If we look at these three origin stories with the eyes of the tracker, listening not to the certainty of their words, not to the visible and literal fabric of story but for the echoes of alienation beneath, we can hear politics in this last contest: two ways of life come up against one another. Cain, as I have noted in Digging out the Taproot of Supremacy, is related etymologically (in Aramaic) to kain, which means 'forge' or 'smith'. Cain is a farmer, a settled agrarian, but also a metal worker. He is a city dweller and a bronze-age smith: he is forging metal tools to work the field, and likely forging swords. He kills his brother. Yet this contest is not merely familial: it is a conflict between ways of life. We have abandoned the hunter gatherer way of life for the dual modes that have emerged from it. In doing so, we have deviated from the original pattern: e.g., Small Band Hunter Gatherers are the baseline of human normalcy.1 We have now embarked on the accelerating deviation from the ancestral baseline that will bring us into the modern era.

Not content to follow the animals, the hunters have become shepherds, keeping the animals close. Not content to follow the fruiting trees, the gatherers have become farmers, keeping the plants close and on a schedule. And these modes of living are giving rise to social orders: nomadic tribal peoples moving with herds and city dwellers storing up grain, the habit of which will soon give birth to property boundaries, numeracy and literacy: the territorial expansion of the abstract, the earliest rootings of domination.

Our way of life and modes of being are in flux: from I move, therefore I am (the small band hunter gatherer center of gravity, knowing ourselves through movement in seasonal rhythm across a landscape) in the direction of the more stationary and abstract I think therefore I am. The sense of self that arises from I move therefore I am is an embodied self, motional, knowing through feeling and sensation: a largely autonomic self. It is our ancestral self: animal, guttural, gestural, moving within the cadences of patterns of daylight, season, and the circadian and cyclic rhythms of the Living World. This moving self lives outdoors all the time.

As modes of living shift, as we move from small band hunter gathering to herding and farming, as the realm of the abstract mushrooms with concepts like land boundaries and the requirements to document and tally what grain is stored where and who traded how many bushels for how many goats, our center of identity gravity begins to shift, to relocate, to congeal. Not moving, fluid, and permeable, because we no longer know ourselves in relationship to migration, our sense of self begins to thicken, to solidify. This congealing will manifest millenia later in Descartes' assertion that I think, therefore I am.

The path from I move, therefore I am to I think, therefore I am, is in fact a series of dismemberments. We lose access to the freedom of our animal selves, their aboriginal knowing (Fall from the Garden), our linguistic freedom of ability to communicate with All and with one another (Fall from Babel). Here, in the story of Cain and Abel, we are warring out the lifestyles that have replaced hunter gathering. The story of Cain and Abel is a political contest between two ways of living. The urban dwelling farmer cum metal smith kills off the nomadic herding people, and is in the process driven one step further from relatedness. This is called the mark of Cain.

*Titian, Cain Slaying Abel- 1542-1544, Santa Maria della Salute, Venice, Italy. Although the Bible says he does this with a rock, I find this image somehow more compelling, and note that the stick Cain is holding is wielded in two hands like a sword.*

Look at the deep pattern in these stories. They are attempts to explain progressive layers of alienation. They are documents grappling with why we feel farther and farther away from the Source context. The story of Adam and Eve configures this as a sin (and the etymology of sin, in Latin, means 'to ask for pain', in Greek it means to 'miss the mark', in Aramaic it means 'unripe') arising from humanity's desire to eat from the Tree of the Knowledge of Good and Evil. Bullshit. It is a story about moving from migratory rhythms we shared with animals into stationary settings. To do this we gave up the balance between masculine and feminine, disowning the wild mother. To do this we gave up our animal natures, disowning the Indigenous.

The opening salvo of the Bible is not what it seems. It is written by people who are already alienated, and casting back for a reason: How did things get to be this way? What it fails utterly to confront is that the baseline of human normalcy is small band hunter gathering. The Original Sin was giving up this ancestral mode of living. What caused us to be ejected from the Garden was that we stopped living in a manner and prioritizing the ways of knowing required to relate.

The Original Sin was giving up living in a manner that prioritized ways of knowing required to relate.

The story of Cain and Abel then situates us in the lineage of murderers, of fratricides, people who have killed our brothers. We are first the descendants of the people thrown out of the garden, then the descendants of murderers. But who are the brothers we killed off? It was a lifestyle that was murdered, not a person. Or not merely a person.

I write to understand myself, what I know, what I feel: to grapple with, to wrestle with, to unearth, unmask, descend, dig into. I write the way a farmer digs furrows into which to plant seeds. It is a visceral full-body act. I don't have time for pontification: don't give a fuck about it. I don't give a fuck what most people think. I don't have time for the abstract, the unanchored, the speculative. I write from my feet. I write from callouses. I write from the earth. I write now to cut open the festering wound. I write as a surgeon.

These essays, however broad in their span, are also personal. I write them because I have to, because I need a way to set things out and survey them, hold them up to the light, examine. These essays in particular, on the death cult, I would rather not be writing. I'd rather be tending the forest, or writing about rainbows and fucking unicorns. But I can't, because I need a vector, a vehicle through which to process the upwellings of crazy that mount in these days, with a criminal fascist madman seeking the US presidency, hawking Bibles, convinced he is a goddam messiah.

I write this particular essay in the wake of a suicide. As a wake for a suicide, perhaps: a liturgical elegy. A form of vigil for someone who might have been me. Now that I've said it, broken the surface tension, now that it is out on the page my attention is drawn, for the first time, to the plants in a vase on the table where I am writing, to scars in the skin of this succulent before me: damage to the leaf. I swim up out of the page for a moment, out of the words and my eyes dwell on the injury.

We've gotten very deeply confused about something spiritual: tangled in it. This tangle has eaten now, extinguished, a number of young men that I know. Four and counting... I was almost one of them, escaped that fate by a hair's breadth.

Here is a way of stating the problem. Modernity, because it is so alienated, has constrained the doorways back to the Source context into the body of a person. We have affixed and located the Source in a man who we call Jesus. Nevermind that we do not understand Him, that we have categorically mis-translated everything he said, and are doomed to do so until we can resurrect the language (Aramaic) and the worldview from which he spoke, nevermind that not even the Church he nominally started (which was later co-opted by Rome) can agree on the most basic fucking facts about the man, nevermind that arguments about his meanings have been debated since he was alive, nevermind that entire segments of his teaching were elided because they did not concord with patriarchy. Nevermind that he himself never claimed to be God. That he kept saying Look through me, pray as I pray, regard the Source context itself...

We have fallen out of relating, which is horizontal, and been acculturated to alienation, which is vertical, because we live in a domination paradigm. We have been socialized into a domination paradigm. The death cult is a domination paradigm. A domination paradigm is a tower, a hierarchy. It has a top. And at the top we have placed, in our alienated ignorance, Jesus. Despite that what seemed to characterize him most deeply was humility. We use him, like most things taken out of context, where he is useful to us. We put Jesus where, in the architecture of our distortion and madness, we need him to go. We use him to spackle over inward emptiness, infill guilt. Use him as spiritual silly putty, mortar, and adhesive. Claim any number of batshit lunacies in his name. The crusades, for example. The Inquisition. Colonialism, for example.

Because, again through our mistranslation, we believe that Jesus said, "I am the Way," we seek to emulate him. This emulation is not done merely by Christians. This emulation is a grand psychic architecture: a pyramid scheme of colossal scale, an Empire building and empire enforcement technology. We come colonizing and we plant crosses.

Here's a macabre joke: The Indians planted corn, and harvested corn. Christians planted crosses. What do they harvest?

The answer is, as you know, genocide. Where we plant religion, we harvest genocide.

Jesus was appointed mascot of the Empire, first of the Roman by the Emperor Theodosius in 380 CE, which sent the actual followers of the teachings running for the hills, then 1500 years later that which is called the United States by its Founding Fathers. Jesus is God of the Republic, God of the Republican Party: the presumptive republican candidate has just become, literally, a Bible salesman.2 Jesus presides, we are told, over this great country, let us make America great again, let us make America pray again. Jesus Jesus Jesus we call as we commit unspeakable and genocidal acts.

> *First negro I struck was this evening for laughing at prayers.*
>
> *—Diary of a Plantation Owner, Havana, 1833*

Jesus, we are conditioned to believe, is the missing piece, the keystone architecture, the fragment of soul that must be plugged into the empty place in us, socketed, the hole in our bodies where the original relating is missing. Jesus, we are told, is the shape of the absence in ourselves, the place we cannot feel or know ourselves.

The problem, the entanglement, as it were, psychically, psychedelically, is that a side effect of this configuration is that when men with a certain awareness of the wound, and a certain kind of sensitivity, begin to have certain kinds of spiritual experiences, birth or rebirth certain kinds of ancestral abilities– to be able to converse with animals, to be able to read signs and signals in the weather– begin to wake up shamanically to the original rhythms, begin to fill the hole, we start to think we are Jesus. Jesus becomes entangled in the awakening. We conceive of Jesus as the Source and when we begin to encounter the Source and merge we put his face on it.

We are drawn, gravitionally, and ineluctably, in this direction. But here's the problem: You ain't Jesus, bruh.

Let's start with an obvious example of who ain't Jesus. A man confronting ninety-one felony cases, including fraud, defamation, sexual assault, hush money, willful retention of national security information, obstruction of justice, witholding of documents, false statements, conspiracy to steal an election, inciting rebellion, etc. is not Jesus. That man is not Jesus. But he thinks he is. He really does.

So how does someone who has made a business out of breaking 9 of the ten commandments, come to believe– I think Trump genuinely believes this– that he is Jesus? And the answer is schizophrenia.

The schizophrenia of supremacy. The answer is that the physics of domination, the way that it organizes psyches, is to break them into two parts, along the same lines that the Tower of Babel was broken: one psychic fragment of tower (an exaltation) that contains all of the perfections (the Jesus attributes) and one psychic fragment of cavern (a depression) that contains all of the imperfections (the Satanic attributes) and to localize the person in only one part of this schizoid formation. The Schizophrenia of Supremacy grasps onto the tower and holds on for dear life. We who are deeply damaged grab hold of the exalted parts of self, and try to make it do the full work of our identity.

The other part, the part that holds all the failures, all the fuckups, all the horrific shit– well that part gets exiled. It becomes enshadowed. It is downward: a cavern. If we travel down into this depression we get, you guessed it, depressed. And we don't tolerate that very well, and so it is ejected and we paint it onto the bodies of other people. The project of supremacy is to exteroject our evil onto the bodies of others. This is how I enslave people and then straight-facedly kneel down in church. How I (the white plantation owner) strike the enslaved negro for laughing at prayers.

Supremacy is the projection of my evil onto others.

White Supremacy is the projection of white evil onto Black bodies.

Male Supremacy is the project of male evil onto female bodies.

The reason that Trump cannot ever – is structurally and categorically unable- to admit that he has made a mistake is because he is perfect. Didn't you know? He is Jesus. He is infallible. A golden God. The parts of him that are corrupted– that fuck pornstars out of wedlock, grab women by the pussy, subvert elections, inflate his net worth, incite violence, summon apocalyptic violence in coded word salad of plausible deniability, use his state office for personal gain, steal, etc etc do not exist despite their reality, because they are incongruent with his self-perception as perfection embodied and because he is superior.

As insane as this sounds (it is insane, in the distillate meaning of that word), it is the archetypal expression of modernity. He is our loudest and most prophetic poet of the death cult, its evangelist: Donald J.

The antidote to the Donald, the antidote to the suicides of which I was nearly one, is to reabsorb our own evil. And in order to do this, we have to understand the physics whereby it got created. The evil was born the moment we decided that we were superior. Or, said slightly differently, our reaction to shame–when I say our reaction, I am speaking mytho-poetically about Adam, and Cain, and all of the ancestors who gave birth to European modernity– was to, rather than humble ourselves and grieve, humble ourselves and lay down at the feet of the Mother, which is Nature, rather than to repent our arrogance, to cradle our own broken hearts and seek to mend them, was to declare ourselves above Nature.

We caused harm– I don't know exactly what this original harm was–but men did this, and so I can speculate, and rather than lay ourselves down at the feet of the Mother and accept the punishment we justly deserved, having broken a sacred trust, we granted ourselves authority over the sovereign bodies of others. We broke the village, the ancestral village, which was horizontal, and in a circle around the fire, the Original Fire– a village where we understood that the Source, the Sacred, was Qadash3: the centerpoint (Qd) and the circle of Light and Heat radiating from it (Ash). We rebelled, turned away, declared ourselves Superior. And since energy is conserved, this push to elevation engendered an equal and opposite force. The act of pushing upwards creates the below. We push heaven up and hell down thusly. That is how it begins. We stopped moving over the land and froze up inside ourselves. This is how it happened, this is what set the process in motion, the schizophrenia of supremacy, from which we can draw a straight line to the modern world.

BOOKS BY NATUREZA GABRIEL

*Transformation through Feeling*
*Restorative Practices of Wellbeing*
*Keywords*
*Can't Get Home*
*The Neurobiology of Connection*
*The Archeology of Shadows*
*Origin Stories for Children*
*Destoryer of Empire (Poems)*

## ABOUT THE AUTHOR

Natureza Gabriel is a connection phenomenologist and neural cartographer. His mind was trained at Yale and Stanford Universities, his heart has been educated in ceremonies and circles. He has spent nearly 30 years studying connection through the lenses of neuroscience, mindful awareness, social justice, deep nature connection, non-cognitive ways of knowing, and cultural linguistics. He is the developer of Autonomics, the principal architect of the Restorative Practices neuro-developmental model, is Host and Executive Producer of *The Restorative Practices Film Series*, and the author of the Connection Phenomenology Series. He is Founder and CEO of Hearth Science: a translation research firm pioneering the union of neurophysiology and ancestral awareness to turn on the deepest drivers of human wellbeing. He teaches as part of a global faculty that he convened, drawn from more than 25 disclines of wellbeing and 24 cultures around the world.

He lives with his family on unceded Miwok territory (Bay Area) in South Salmon Nation (California) on western Turtle Island (United States), where his hobbies include stewarding an eco-reserve and practicing linguistic neurosurgery.

You can find more of his work, as well as that of the extraordinary faculty of Hearth Science at:

HTTPS://restorativepractices.com

www.ingramcontent.com/pod-product-compliance
Lightning Source LLC
Chambersburg PA
CBHW031149020426
42333CB00013B/575